CONTENTS

FOREWORD

Rural England is a place of great beauty and diversity. The countryside is one of our country's most valuable assets and something to be enjoyed by all. The Government wants to make sure that rural areas will continue to be places where people want to live, work and enjoy leisure. For this to happen we need those areas to have a strong local economic base that can sustain vibrant communities and nurture a high-quality rural environment. Nowhere are the principles of sustainable development more important: economic prosperity must go hand in hand with the protection of the rural environment and be for the benefit of rural communities and the nation as a whole.

Economic, environmental and social factors have combined to create profound changes in rural England over recent years. Yet, in spite of these changes, little attention has been paid to defining the Government's overall objectives for rural economies, to reviewing the underlying rationale for government intervention in rural economies or to assessing the adequacy of the existing policy framework. That is why the Prime Minister asked the Performance & Innovation Unit (PIU) to undertake a study of rural economies.

The PIU project, for which I was the Sponsor Minister, has identified a mismatch between the existing policy framework (rooted in the realities of the late 1940s) and new views on what the countryside is for. The PIU believes there is a need to modernise the policy framework so that Government efforts are focused on encouraging and supporting the creation of productive, sustainable and inclusive rural economies. The PIU argues that the Government should be aiming for a rural England with enterprising economies, a sustainable agriculture, an enhanced environment and thriving communities. The PIU concludes that, for this to be achieved, there will need to be changes not only to the Government's objectives but also to the detail of policy on a number of issues.

What those changes should be is a proper matter for wide public debate. The PIU has researched the issues in considerable depth and come to some far-reaching conclusions. These conclusions are offered not as a statement of Government policy but rather as a further contribution to the debate on how best to reform policy. Many ideas have already been submitted to the Government in response to the consultation on *Rural England*, the discussion document published in February 1999. These responses have been fed into the development work on the Rural White Paper. We want the new arguments, analysis and conclusions in this report to take that development work further and to continue to extend the discussion of the issues beyond the 'Whitehall Village'. So we would welcome responses from readers with a professional or personal interest in the new issues raised in the report. The report highlights a series of 'issues for discussion' (pages 14–16) on which the Government would particularly welcome views.

Public debate on these issues is not an optional extra that can be bolted on to policy-making: it is an essential part of forming a new and effective set of responses to the challenges that rural areas face. I believe that, working together, the Government and the people of this country can ensure that the English countryside remains a source of wealth, beauty and pride. I hope that the PIU report will help achieve this goal.

Rt Hon Andrew Smith MP
Chief Secretary to the Treasury

1. EXECUTIVE SUMMARY

1.1   Rural England matters. Using the broadest definition of rurality, it is home to up to a quarter of the nation's population, containing a diversity of communities within which people live and work. And it accounts for over 80% of the land mass, containing landscapes and places of great beauty and environmental value. Whether they live in town or country, what English people value most about the countryside is the quality of the rural environment and the social fabric of rural communities. Rural economies[1] matter not just because of the contribution they make to national wealth, but also because they are the foundation for these social and environmental outcomes.

1.2   Rural economies differ from area to area. When statistics are aggregated, rural economies appear similar to their urban counterparts in many ways. Importantly, for both urban and rural economies, policies with a national sweep – whether instituted by the Government or the EU – have a much greater impact on economic health than any specific urban or rural-tailored initiative. But the differences between urban and rural areas – the role of agriculture, and the rural landscapes and habitats – are sufficient to require a distinctive "rural policy". In determining rural policy, the Government needs to be mindful of the strengths of rural economies – the quality-of-life benefits, the environmental, social and cultural resources, the potential competitive advantages such as proximity to natural resources – as well as their weaknesses, which are largely related

to population sparsity and distance from urban centres.

Rural policy and the changing countryside

1.3   The current framework for rural policy has its roots in the late 1940s. At that time, the government had a clear view of what the countryside was for, and could command a wide consensus in support of this view. It saw agriculture as the primary function of rural areas and, therefore, as their key economic sector; and it viewed agriculture's primary role as to ensure security of food supply. It assumed that farmers, as the stewards and shapers of 'the countryside', could be relied upon to protect the quality of the rural environment. It assumed that the shift of population from rural to urban areas would continue, and therefore that the greatest threat to the rural environment would be around the fringes of urban areas. And it believed that rising output from agriculture and other primary sectors in rural areas, combined with universal models of public service provision, would generate sufficient wealth to tackle rural poverty. All of these views were valid at the time and constituted a coherent framework for rural policy.

1.4   This framework was supported by a consistent set of instruments, leading to notable successes. The government intervened heavily in the agriculture sector to encourage the expansion of domestic food production, introducing price support,

[1] The diversity across the country makes it inappropriate to think of a single 'rural economy', separate from and different to economic activity in urban areas.

production subsidies and special treatment for farmers within the tax and land-use planning systems. In relation to the environment, the government introduced restrictions on any development in what were viewed as the most valuable sites – National Parks, Areas of Outstanding Natural Beauty and Green Belt land – with less protection for other sites (including some with high biodiversity or habitat value). And the government viewed universal provision of public services in or close to all settlements as an affordable and effective way of meeting social needs. Taken together, these policies contributed to the spectacular growth in agricultural productivity and output, restricted urban sprawl and ensured that rural people had access to the welfare state.

1.5   But the values, beliefs and behaviours on which post-war policy was based have not proved to be permanent. Social and economic trends have combined to produce a fundamental change in views of what the countryside is for and in values and priorities for public policy. Public concern about food has shifted from issues of quantity to issues of quality (notably safety). There has been a marked increase in levels of interest in and concern for the environment, so that many people now value rural England more as a source of environmental goods than as a place for food production. More and more people want to live in the countryside and to enjoy the leisure and recreational opportunities it offers. And a growing consensus has emerged that rural areas are appropriate for more than just land-based economic activity. In addition, mobility and social trends have combined to weaken many of the traditional self-support systems within rural communities. And a demand for higher quality services, allied to a reluctance to pay higher prices and taxes – has brought into question the viability of universal models of service provision in all locations.

1.6   Since the 1970s there has been a series of incremental reforms to the policy framework (with the scope for national autonomy significantly reduced since the UK's entry into the Common Market), in part to reflect these changes in circumstances, values and priorities. But in spite of these changes, much of the framework developed immediately after the Second World War remains largely intact. There is continuing heavy intervention in agricultural production – and the industry still experiences special treatment in some areas of public policy (for example, land-use planning), as well as being unique in retaining a near-dedicated Whitehall ministry in the form of the Ministry of Agriculture, Fisheries and Food (MAFF). There is continuing reliance on a small number of land-use planning devices, furnished for the world of the late 1940s, to manage the potential tensions between conservation and development in rural areas. And there is a continuing emphasis on delivering services from within organisational and departmental 'silos', even though such approaches are often uneconomic, inefficient and ineffective. In short, there is a mismatch between the reality of the English countryside today and the inherited policy framework (rooted in the realities and policy instruments of the late 1940s).

Problems facing rural economies

1.7   Rural economies in England are experiencing a number of problems, and while some rural communities continue to prosper, others are experiencing problems of economic adjustment. Although most of these problems stem from broad social, technological and economic changes which go far beyond national boundaries, the national policy framework can contribute to some of these and can prevent the resolution of others. Some rural areas and some sectors of rural economies have experienced problems of structural adjustment, while others face limits on dynamism and diversification. Although agricultural output has been rising, its shares of employment and Gross Domestic Product (GDP) have been falling relative to other sectors, and agriculture faces a current mixture of cyclical and structural difficulties, yet still consumes extensive (and increasing) amounts of public money on production-related payments. The quality of the environment in many parts of rural England has suffered in the face of intensive farming and the shift of population from urban to rural areas, often generating sharp tensions between conservation and development. Poverty in rural areas is a significant and persistent problem, and there are rising problems of access to transport and key services for a minority of rural people.

1.8 In short, rural life is changing, as rural areas are subject to the impact of big social and economic forces. Government cannot stop these forces: but it can influence some of the changes and help rural areas to adjust.

The need for change

1.9 Without change to policy, these problems and tensions may worsen, with potentially damaging consequences for some rural areas. Forecasts suggest that, without new policies, rural areas will continue to experience economic difficulties and a decline in the quality of the environment. And, perhaps more dramatically, the UK agriculture sector will face major challenges as a result of trade liberalisation, globalisation and EU enlargement. In short, the status quo is not an option. The policy framework is in need of modernisation.

A new policy framework

1.10 A new policy framework will need to be based upon:

- *economic insights into what government can and should do.* The Government has a key role in meeting social, environmental and economic goals. Specifically, it can help preserve and improve the quality of life for rural people, the economic opportunities for rural communities and the character and accessibility of the countryside. There is broad agreement that Government action should focus on tackling market failures and pursuing the Government's distributional objectives; but it is important to recognise the costs of intervention and the fact that governments as well as markets can fail;

- *evidence about the problems of rural areas that new policies will need to address.* There is broad agreement (reflected in the analysis outlined above) about many of the problems faced by rural areas; and

- perhaps most importantly, *a clear and coherent vision for the future of the countryside,* which can command consensus. There is broad support for the five principles outlined in the Government's recent Rural White Paper consultation document 'Rural England':

- a belief in a living countryside;

- a belief in a working countryside;

- a recognition of the interdependence of town and country;

- a commitment to protect the rural environment and enhance its qualities;

- a belief that the countryside should be accessible to all.

1.11 The Government can build on these areas of agreement, and on its overall national economic objectives, by adopting the following aim and set of objectives for rural economies:

Overall aim:

To encourage and support the creation of productive, sustainable and inclusive rural economies

Objectives:

1. To facilitate the development of dynamic and competitive rural economies – in particular, through:

   a) tackling the market and government failures that hamper rural economies

   b) encouraging the operation of market forces in the agriculture sector, tempered by action to ensure good and safe practice and the supply of public goods

2. To ensure that economic dynamism is environmentally sustainable (in part through pursuing the objective for the agriculture sector, outlined at 1b above)

3. To ensure more equitable access to economic & social opportunities in rural areas

A future for rural economies

1.12 With these objectives driving policy, it is possible to envisage a rural England in 2010 with the following features and characteristics:

1.13 *An enterprising countryside:* Government policy and market dynamism will combine to stimulate enterprise, wealth generation and growth in rural England – providing economic strength and security for communities in the countryside. There will be:

- a reduced burden of regulation on rural businesses;
- an improved planning system, more supportive of the needs of rural businesses, as well as of wider planning objectives;
- an enrichment of the skills base of rural economies;
- improved infrastructure in rural areas;
- improved provision of advice and support services for rural businesses;
- improved support for the tourism and recreation sectors.

1.14 *Sustainable agriculture:* England will enjoy an agricultural industry that can compete, survive and thrive in the 21st century – with farmers able to adapt and diversify their businesses to reflect market demand and their sources of commercial advantage. The primary economic role of agriculture will continue to be the production of food: but farmers will be better positioned to deliver the range of environmental outputs valued by society. There will be:

- a reduced dependence of farmers on production subsidies (with a commensurate reduction in government expenditure) but an increased level of support for farmers' contribution to the environment;
- a move towards a level playing-field for agriculture and other sectors of rural economies;
- a reduction in red tape and an improved range of business advice and support services for farmers, making it easier to diversify and develop farm businesses;

- a continuation of the process of restructuring, creating more efficient farms, with greater potential to sustain employment in the longer term;

- a diversity of competitive strategies pursued by farmers, with a focus on new and emerging markets (such as that for organic food);

- an improved relationship between farmers and their customers – so that farmers provide more of what the public wants in the way the public wants it;

- a programme of more extensive reform within the EU, which the UK will have played a central role in shaping and driving.

1.15 *An enhanced environment:* England's rural environment will remain a source of beauty, wealth and pride – with more resources and greater protection for what we value most in the English countryside. There will be:

- a rise in the level of environmentally friendly practice across the agriculture industry;

- protection for the land of greatest environmental value from inappropriate development;

- improved land-use planning in rural areas, with more open and better-informed debates at the start of the planning process about the needs of an area, and about how to balance economic and environmental objectives – debates that will engage the whole of a local community, not just the vociferous minorities;

- stronger, more transparent mechanisms to limit and compensate for any damage to the rural environment caused by development;

- better management of local traffic;

- improved access to the countryside for people from both rural and urban areas.

1.16 *Thriving and inclusive communities:* Rural England will retain living, working communities with improved access to services and resources. There will be:

- stronger rural economies, providing opportunities for wealth creation and employment that are necessary for the vitality of rural communities;

- improved access to public, community and commercial transport services;

- improved access to public and private services in rural areas – with public bodies encouraged to pool resources and make greater use of mobile provision, and through new ways of harnessing the power of information and communications technologies (ICT) to overcome problems of distance and sparsity;

- more effective targeting of services to address social and economic problems;

- improved provision of social and affordable housing in rural areas as part of a commitment to sustaining balanced communities;

- a strengthening of market towns as centres of economic activity and service delivery.

The agenda for action

1.17 Statements of vision and objectives are necessary for an effective response by government to the economic problems and opportunities of rural areas; but they are not sufficient. The new framework must be supported by a set of policies, processes and instruments that give practical effect to the objectives, shifting the focus from 'where do we want to go?' to 'how do we get there?'

The objectives generate a need for action in four main areas:

- *economic policy* – where the imperative should be to encourage prosperity and wealth creation;

- *environmental policy* – where the imperative should be to equip government to sustain and enhance the rural environment;

- *agricultural policy* – where the imperative should be to develop a competitive, forward-looking, modernised industry; and

- *social policy* – where the imperative should be to forge a new commitment to rural communities.

1.18 Membership of the EU means the Government cannot act alone. In a number of key policy areas – of which agricultural support is the most important – the Government can only make progress by working with EU partners. This is not always easy. Nevertheless, a programme of reform of the Common Agricultural Policy (CAP) was agreed at the Berlin Summit earlier this year, which provides valuable opportunities for national discretion; and there are also significant opportunities for national responses to a range of economic, environmental, agricultural and social issues.

Economic policy: encouraging an enterprising countryside

1.19 To implement its objective of facilitating dynamic and competitive rural economies, the Government will need to combine a general presumption in favour of market forces with positive policies for the problems that it can and should seek to resolve.

1.20 In part, the challenge for the Government is to find better ways of

shaping and influencing economic activity in rural areas. There are opportunities to make the planning system more supportive of an enterprising countryside without jeopardising the rural environment, by striking a better balance between local deliberative processes and national regulations. Such an approach would allow the removal of unnecessary national regulations and guidance in order to facilitate changes of commercial use, farm diversification and the conversion of redundant buildings for commercial purposes (although care needs to be taken to ensure that changes are in accordance with the principles of sustainable development). Moreover, the special treatment of agriculture within the planning system (in particular, the national protection for the 'Best and Most Versatile' – BMV – agricultural land) needs to be re-assessed against current thinking – in particular, the desirability of protecting land of high environmental value. Making the removal of protection for BMV land dependent on the introduction of a new national framework for protecting land of high environmental value could provide reassurance and constitute a significant improvement on the current system of BMV protection. And, more generally, the Government may wish to review the impact of other forms of business regulation in rural economies – notably in the agriculture and food-processing sectors, but more generally for small and micro-businesses.

1.21 But the Government should also tackle those market failures that it has shown itself to be capable of correcting. First, how to enrich the skills base of the workforce in rural areas, particularly where there is significant economic adjustment out of primary industries. Second, how to improve the infrastructure in rural areas, both in terms of telecommunications as well as transport links and business sites. Third, how to improve the quality and reach of business advice and support in rural areas, with a particular focus on integrating advice from different sources for farmers to assist them in diversification and on making the Small Business Service work effectively in rural areas.

1.22 Finally, while the Government should avoid heavy involvement in any particular sector of rural economies, there is a case for it to play a more proactive role in the development of the tourism and recreation industries by funding integrating facilities, financing improvements to rural tourist infrastructure and encouraging the development of regional tourism and recreation strategies.

Environmental policy: equipping government to sustain and enhance the rural environment

1.23 What is meant by 'the environment' changes over time – and so does what is valued within the environment. Currently, many people value not merely the rural landscape and its natural resources but also biodiversity and the historical features of rural settings. There is also a growing recognition that society should value and protect environmental attributes in all of these categories, and that countryside policy should be concerned with access as well as conservation. The policy framework needs to be modernised to reflect this new consensus and equip government to sustain and enhance the rural environment.

1.24 The Government's strategy for the rural environment should be based on the principles of sustainability, subsidiarity and flexibility. These broad principles can be

turned into practicable policies only if the Government is adequately informed about developments and trends within the rural environment and if options and choices are brought into focus by the specifics of environmental indicators and targets. The Government, in conjunction with regional and local authorities, should review the adequacy of its information base and its use of performance indicators and targets to inform environmental strategies and policies.

1.25 The effective implementation of environmental strategies requires government to develop a broader range of policy instruments. The Government should continue to review and revise the land-use planning system to ensure that it is able to deliver policies for the countryside. There is a need for local authorities to make greater use of deliberative processes – such as the preparation of village design statements – through which local people can help shape the future of their areas. And options for the development of new policy instruments – for example, offsetting mechanisms and impact charges – should be considered.

1.26 In addition to modernising its approach to planning, the Government should consider further reforms to realise its environmental objectives. It should continue to undertake research into the feasibility of a new national framework for protecting land of high environmental value. And it should consider redirecting resources within existing rural programmes (principally, those for agricultural support and rural regeneration) towards schemes that protect and enhance the environment, while at the same time creating new economic opportunities.

Agricultural policy: developing a competitive, forward-looking, modernised industry

1.27 Rural England needs a vibrant and competitive agriculture industry, not merely as a source of employment and wealth but also as the principal means of managing the rural environment. The Government can help the industry to become more competitive; and it can take steps to ensure that farmers produce the environmental goods that are valued by society. But agricultural policy is in need of modernisation if these objectives are to be realised.

1.28 While the CAP is a major constraint on the Government's ability to modernise, the recent Agenda 2000 deal at the Berlin Summit offers increased national discretion to deploy CAP resources – through the new Rural Development Regulation (RDR) – to meet environmental and rural development objectives. Member States can redirect additional resources to the RDR by 'modulating'[2] a proportion (up to one-fifth) of the compensation payments that are paid to farmers as a result of the 1992 and 1999 CAP reforms. Modulation should be considered as a way of redirecting resources away from production-related payments towards measures that enhance the countryside, such as agri-environment schemes (which help agriculture to maintain and enhance valued environmental goods).

1.29 In addition, the Government should explore two other opportunities for national discretion to improve agriculture's contribution to the rural environment. First, making all direct CAP payments conditional upon compliance with a set of minimum standards for good environmental practice.

Second, refocusing additional support for farmers in Less Favoured Areas on a new agri-environment land management programme – with production-related Hill Livestock Compensatory Allowances phased out as this new agri-environment programme for the hills is phased in.

1.30 The Government should reform domestic policy on agriculture to encourage a diversity of competitive strategies in the industry, giving farmers the chance to operate other than simply as low-cost, high-volume commodity producers. Through a combination of measures the Government can assist the growth of the organic sector, the spread of farmers' markets, the development of technological innovations and the expansion of locally differentiated and branded produce. Over the longer term, the competitiveness of the agriculture industry – and the workings of rural economies more generally – will be better served by placing farmers on a level playing field with other businesses.

1.31 In considering these ideas for reforms over the short and medium-term, the Government should not lose sight of the biggest prize: fundamental reform of the CAP. Without European-wide reform the major barriers to agricultural competitiveness, good environmental practice and value for money will persist. It is therefore essential that the Government continues to take a lead in Europe, shaping the arguments and building the alliances among Member States that will make CAP reform a reality. This will require persistence and determination over many years.

---

[2] Reallocating CAP funds from compensation payments to other agriculture-related programmes.

Social policy: a new commitment to rural communities

1.32 A new commitment to rural communities will require:

● innovative approaches to service delivery;

● within the overall new commitment to rural communities, a specific commitment to Market Towns (the settlements that constitute the key nodes for much economic activity and service delivery in rural areas);

● improved access to public, private, commercial and voluntary transport; and

● a recognition of the importance of affordable and social housing in achieving the Government's economic, environmental and social objectives for rural England.

1.33 It is possible to question the affordability and effectiveness of the post-war model of service delivery, in which each separate government body and department attempted to maintain its own dispersed network of service outlets in or close to almost every settlement. Rather than persist with outdated approaches, Government organisations should: join up their efforts, looking for opportunities to establish multi-functional outlets; make greater use of mobile provision; and explore the role that information and communications technology (ICT) can play in allowing the electronic delivery of services to more remote settlements.

1.34 The Government should consider introducing a new commitment to market towns, recognising the key role these settlements play in rural economies and rural communities. This commitment could be realised in part by more effective integration of the wide range of existing initiatives and in part by the introduction of new initiatives (such as the piloting of Business Improvement Districts in market towns). Regional Development Agencies (RDAs) should ensure that market towns are addressed explicitly in their regional economic strategies and should work in partnership with local authorities, business representatives and others to pilot the new commitment.

1.35 Transport policy for rural areas must recognise that the private car will remain the most important means of transport for many journeys: the Government should consider targeting support to increase access by certain groups (e.g. people within the New Deal) to private transport. Public transport has a key role to play in improving access and reducing dependence on the private car in rural areas; but service improvements take time to generate increases in use, so the Government should avoid funding decisions that create significant fluctuations in the provision of public transport.

1.36 Rural housing policy should be a major focus for the Rural White Paper and the Housing Green Paper. But the broad principles of the Government's strategy can be identified at this stage: it needs to improve the provision of social and affordable housing in rural areas while ensuring that development pressures do not destroy what is valued most about rural England – the quality of its environment. Without adequate provision of social and affordable housing, large parts of rural England risk becoming the near-exclusive preserve of the more affluent sections of society. This risk poses an important challenge to the goal of achieving balanced communities.

Conclusion

1.37 The ideas and suggestions in this report could constitute the most substantial and positive set of reforms to rural policy in the last 50 years. They would:

- ensure more effective use of government money in rural areas;

- address the concerns of rural communities – in terms of jobs and economic prosperity, the quality of the environment and access to services;

- look to the future and allow the inevitable processes of adjustment – especially in the agriculture sector – to be managed effectively; and

- preserve and protect what is valued most about rural England.

1.38 By rejecting the option of 'more of the same' in favour of change, the Government would be able not merely to modernise one of the last unreformed parts of the post-war settlement. It would also be able to ensure that rural areas remain a source of wealth, beauty and pride – not just for those who live in rural England, but for the nation as a whole.

Issues for Discussion

1. The vision, aim and objectives for rural economies. (ch 6)

2. Ways of enhancing the skills base of rural economies. How these should be funded. The roles of RDAs and the University for Industry. (ch 7)

3. Ways of developing the infrastructure of rural areas (e.g. telecommunications and transport) to encourage economic growth. How the government should ensure that its policies on transport infrastructure best support rural communities. (ch 7)

4. Ways of providing (and funding) extra support to rural businesses. How to ensure that the Small Business Service will be as effective in rural areas as in urban areas. (ch 7)

5. How the Government can further support tourism and recreation sectors in rural areas. The roles of RDAs and the English Tourism Council in providing this support. (ch 7)

6. How the Government can ensure that its policies on business regulation are sensitive to the needs of rural areas. The case for special arrangements to reflect the needs of small and micro businesses. The case for further investigation of regulation in the agriculture and food processing sectors with a view to identifying opportunities to reduce the regulatory burden. (ch 7)

7. How the planning framework can be used to assist economic development and diversification while avoiding development that rural areas cannot sustain. Within rural planning processes, the correct balance between national guidance and local discretion. How to strengthen local deliberative processes. What restrictions on economic development in rural areas should be lifted. (ch 7)

8. The case for including agricultural development fully within planning control arrangements on the same basis as other commercial development in the countryside. (ch 7)

9. The case for changing the presumption against development of Best and Most Versatile agricultural land. In any process of change, how the Government can ensure that it establishes appropriate protection for land of high environmental value. (ch 7)

10. In order to sustain and enhance the rural environment, how to encourage and enable greater use of local appraisal techniques, strengthen the Local Agenda 21 process and facilitate the operation of community-led environmental schemes. (ch 8)

11. The form and content of a new framework for identifying and ensuring appropriate protection for rural land of high environmental value. (ch 8)

12. The potential for introducing off-setting mechanisms and/or a standardised system of impact charges to capture the full effects of development proposals. (ch 8)

13. The case for introducing modulation of CAP compensation payments, with the resources used for environmental and rural policy objectives. If introduced, the form that the policy should take. (ch 9)

14. The desirability of a significant expansion of agri-environment schemes, and a recasting over the longer term of the various schemes to reduce administrative costs and maximise public benefits. (ch 9)

15. Whether (and if so how) the Government should apply cross-compliance conditions within the national operation of the CAP, as a means of pursuing its policy objectives for the rural environment. (ch 9)

16. The case for moving, over time, from a system that provides additional support to farms in Less Favoured Areas (LFAs) on a production basis towards a system in which any additional support would be wholly conditional on participation in agri-environment management agreements. (ch 9)

17. Ways in which the Government can change domestic policy to improve the competitiveness of the agriculture sector: for example, a time-limited expansion of the Organic Aid Scheme to assist with conversion costs, a review of barriers to farmers' markets and the encouragement of collaborative purchasing and marketing arrangements. (ch 9)

18. How the Government can continue to press for fundamental reform of the Common Agricultural Policy. (ch 9)

19. How the Government should promote innovative approaches to service delivery in rural areas. (ch 9)

20. The desirability of a new commitment to Market Towns, involving the integration of existing rural initiatives and the introduction of new initiatives – for example, Business Improvement Districts. (ch 9)

21. How to improve access to public, private and voluntary transport in rural areas. (ch 9)

22. How the Government can reflect the importance of affordable and social housing for rural areas in its forthcoming policy proposals for housing reform. (ch 9)

Comments on these issues, and on other matters of interest raised by the report, should be sent by February 11th 2000 to:

The Rural White Paper Team
DETR
Zone 3/A5
Eland House
Bressenden Place
LONDON SW1E 5DU

2. BACKGROUND TO THE PIU STUDY

Introduction

2.1   Economic activity in English rural areas has been subject to considerable change in recent decades. There has been a continuing decline in the economic contribution of agriculture and other primary industries throughout rural areas and a (geographically uneven) growth in newer, often service sector, types of employment.

2.2   Rural areas and economies are likely to face further substantial changes in the future, as pressures for reform of the Common Agricultural Policy (CAP) continue, as processes of economic restructuring and technological change alter the spatial configuration of economic activity, and as the processes of population deconcentration and growth in the number of households continue to unfold. In addition to these social and economic issues, public debate and concern over environmental issues has grown markedly over the last 25 years. Together, these economic, social and environmental factors have created a dynamic process of rapid change in rural England – though the manifestations of this change vary significantly from area to area. As a result, rural England is experiencing a complex set of opportunities and problems.

2.3   The work of Government in rural areas is being altered by changes to the operation of the CAP and the establishment of new organisations – notably the Regional Development Agencies and the Countryside Agency. In addition to these reforms, the government is in the process of preparing a Rural White Paper, which will allow a review of existing strategies and policies for English rural areas – including strategies and policies that affect rural economies.

2.4   In spite of the significant nature of the changes experienced in rural England over recent years, little attention has been paid either to defining the Government's overall objectives for rural economies, or to reviewing the underlying rationale for government intervention in rural economies. This contrasts with the process of change underway in the countryside itself. Without a clear and coherent set of objectives, the activities of government run the risk of being predominantly reactive, and influenced by historic models of 'the problem' that no longer fit either the reality of rural areas or the generally accepted view of what the government's role should be in relation to economic matters.

2.5   To explore these issues, the Prime Minister asked the Performance and Innovation Unit to undertake a review of the Government's objectives for rural economies. The project confined its attention to England (though research on examples of good practice extended to other parts of the UK). The PIU project remit was fourfold:

- **to identify the main problems experienced by rural economies in England;**

- **to outline the rationale for government intervention in rural economies;**

- in the light of the government's wider vision for rural areas, the understanding of rural economic problems and the rationale for intervention, **to define a set of objectives for government policies on rural economies in England;**

- **to identify the instruments and organisational arrangements that will allow the government to achieve these objectives most effectively**, and make appropriate recommendations for change to existing government activity.

The context for Government Policy

2.6   The report examines the effectiveness of government policies towards rural economies. However, it is vital to see these policies in a wider context. First, social and economic change over centuries has shaped the countryside we know today, and this change will continue: attempts by government to "stop the clock" would be futile. Second, the Government is only one player amongst many. It is the choices of individuals and communities that matter most. Government may intervene directly, for example on an individual planning decision. It may seek to influence choices, for example by introducing a lower tax rate for less polluting cars. But it is businesses and pressure groups, voluntary bodies and individuals, who make up rural economies. No government could ever "create" a particular rural economy, or direct its operations, any more than it could a rural society or rural environment.

2.7   As an example of this, government spending is typically only 40% of rural economies. The majority of that spending is either determined nationwide (such as defence or social security payments) or only has a limited variation according to local circumstances (such as health or education).

This reflects the fact that the main priorities of rural people are the same as those living in cities or suburbs: health, education, crime and transport. Spending on specifically rural programmes will always be a very small proportion of the total rural economy.

2.8   A further example is provided by the growth of information and communication technology. Governments may set the regulatory framework. They may try to ensure wider access, for example by linking all schools to the internet. They may make use of the technology themselves to introduce new services, such as NHS Direct. These are significant decisions, but the decisions of those who live and work in the countryside matter more. There are millions of choices made by individuals and communities: whether to invest in new equipment, what to study at college, or to rebuild a village hall to include access to the latest technology. Even in farming, where governments have a great deal of direct influence, one of the greatest changes in recent years has been the introduction of the mobile phone.

2.9   As well as being realistic about the role of government, it is important to see rural economies and the wider context in the correct historical background. The English countryside that we know today is almost entirely the product of human action. This can be seen clearly in the pattern of fields and hedges, villages and towns, small woods and green lanes which make up the "classic" English landscape. It is more stark in the open fields of the Fens, which would still lie below the North Sea but for the work of generations of farmers and engineers. Even in the more remote uplands of Cumbria or Devon, the traces of our ancestors can be seen at every turn.

2.10 Many rural people can remember a time when tractors were a rarity. Now, the mechanisation of agriculture has replaced the shire horse and the whole industry they supported, from blacksmiths to horse-dealers. Similar changes mean that, in many villages, farm workers are now a small minority of the population. And as technology has produced larger machines, small fields have become less efficient. Between 1984 and 1990, an estimated 130,000 km of hedgerows in England and Wales were lost.

2.11 Many agricultural sectors have been benefited from years of price support, from the UK government and, since 1973, through the European Union as well. Governments have set prices, supported the expansion of production, allocated quotas, encouraged the planning of particular crops, stored surpluses and subsidised exports. But as world trade becomes more integrated, barriers are being lowered and production and export subsidies reduced with the aim of moving towards market prices. Every farm in England is feeling these effects, as they are in the Netherlands or New Zealand.

2.12 Social changes too have had an enormous impact on the countryside. For example, the last fifty years have seen the creation of a "leisure culture" in the developed world. People work shorter hours and have longer holidays and a greater disposal income. Tourism has overtaken agriculture as the largest employers in many rural areas.

2.13 In short, the countryside has been shaped by powerful economic and social forces which run far beyond the boundaries of a single community, or region, or even country. This process continues, and the PIU team has carried out the project with an appropriate sense of realism about the limited impact that government policies can have.

The Project

2.14 The project, which began in February 1999, was undertaken by a team led by Greg Wilkinson (on secondment from Andersen Consulting) and comprising Neil Ward (on secondment from Newcastle University) and Sarah Thomas (on secondment from the National Assembly for Wales). The team was assisted by Paul O'Sullivan (on secondment from the Department of the Environment, Transport and the Regions) and Stephen Glover (on secondment from HM Treasury) from the PIU's central staff. After consulting widely on a draft project specification, the team's research involved:

- undertaking extensive analysis of existing data and published material;

- holding a series of seminars with specialists in rural, agricultural and economic policy;

- interviewing representatives from a wide range of rural interest groups;

- interviewing officials in Government departments, agencies, and non-departmental, regional and local government bodies;

- undertaking fieldwork in different parts of England and the rest of the UK.

2.15 The project was overseen by the Right Honourable Andrew Smith MP (Chief Secretary to the Treasury, formerly Minister of State at the Department for Education and Employment), who also chaired a steering group of officials and other experts on rural and economic matters. The team benefited considerably from being able to draw on the steering group members' advice and guidance throughout the project. However, responsibility for the final report remains with the PIU.

2.17 Further information on the PIU and its projects and copies of its reports can be found on the PIU website (www.cabinet-office.gov.uk/innovation). Annex A1 of this report contains information about the work of the PIU and membership of the steering group.

3. WHY RURAL ECONOMIES MATTER

Summary

Rural economies matter because they produce economic, environmental and social goods of great value to the nation. Rural areas account for over four-fifths of the land mass and up to a quarter of the population. Rural economies are similar to their urban counterparts in many ways and there are close interrelations between the two. But the differences are sufficiently obvious – the importance of agriculture, the dispersed nature of economic activity, and the rural landscapes and habitats – to justify a distinctive "rural policy". In determining rural policy, Government needs to be mindful of the strengths of rural economies – quality of life benefits, the environmental, social and cultural resources, the potential competitive advantages such as proximity to natural resources – as well as their weaknesses, which are largely related to population sparsity and distance from urban centres.

Introduction

3.1   There are three practical reasons why rural issues should warrant the attention of policy-makers. First, rural England is home to a sizeable minority of the nation's population and contains a diversity of communities within which people live and work. Second, it provides a base for economic activity that contributes to the material wealth of the nation as well as helping to sustain rural communities. And third, it contains landscapes and places of great beauty and environmental value.

3.2   Survey after survey – of both the residents of rural England and their urban counterparts – reveals that what people value most about the countryside is the quality of the rural environment and the social fabric of rural communities. But the economic activity of rural areas underpins these social and environmental outcomes. Without a strong local economic base, many rural communities risk becoming little more than dormitory facilities for urban commuters. And the apparently 'natural' rural environment is the consequence of centuries of human endeavour in land-based economic activities – notably farming, which uses 75% of the land in England. Economic activity shapes the environment – for better or for worse.

3.3   In short, economic matters are central to the overall health and welfare of rural England and to the quality of life experienced by its inhabitants and visitors. This makes it essential that policy-makers have a clear understanding of rural economies – what they are, where they are, how they resemble and differ from the economies of urban areas, their strengths and weaknesses, what activities happen in them and how well they are performing – before determining what contribution the Government should make to the well-being of rural areas. This chapter provides the insights necessary for that understanding.

What do we mean by 'rural economies'?

3.4   As the House of Commons Environment Select Committee observed in its 1996 report on the last Rural White Paper, 'Rurality is a difficult concept'.[1] Any study of economic activity in rural areas will immediately encounter a series of definitional issues that have taxed social scientists for decades. These concern questions of: the definition of rurality; the most appropriate spatial scale of data analysis; and the bounded nature (or otherwise) of economic activity in rural areas. In large part, problems of definition arise because of the marked variation in social, economic and environmental conditions between areas that are commonly regarded – by inhabitants and outsiders – as 'rural'.

3.5   There are no objective answers to these questions. Different parts of government use different definitions for different purposes. Indeed, within central government alone it is possible to identify at least a dozen different definitions of rurality, all currently in active use. Definitions, of course, have a material impact on key indicators.

3.6   The PIU team has taken a pragmatic approach to these questions. It has assessed the definitions (and associated classifications of local authorities) used by the DETR, the Countryside Agency and the National Council for Voluntary Organisations and found there to be substantial common ground between the different views. The definition of rurality used by the former Rural Development Commission – all settlements with populations of less than 10,000 people – is more problematic, as it excludes a number of market towns that are integral to the pattern of economic and social activity in rural areas. But using local authority districts (rather than settlements) as the unit for analysis goes some way towards overcoming this problem.[2] It allows the analyst to operate using the consensus that exists between the different definitions and classifications. This consensus is represented in Map 3.1: it shows 108 districts as 'accessible rural', 63 as 'remote rural' and 10 as former coalfield districts. Together, these authorities constitute rural England for the purposes of the PIU study. They account for over 80% of the land mass and approaching 25% of the population.

3.7   The 'rural economies' under analysis in the PIU project are the sum of the recorded economic activity of individuals and entities in rural areas. Economic activity is used in its broadest sense, to cover:

- markets for goods and services and for labour;

- non-market goods arising from economic and social activity – in particular, the range of environmental goods (biodiversity, species diversity, the appearance of the landscape, amenities etc) arising from land use in rural areas;

- the provision of public services in non-market settings.

[1]   *Rural England* (1996), House of Commons Environment Committee, HMSO.

[2]   Though some districts classified as 'rural' will also contain larger settlements that many people would view as urban, thereby resulting on occasions in a conflation of 'town' and 'country' in the data sets.

Map 3.1 Classification of local authority areas in England

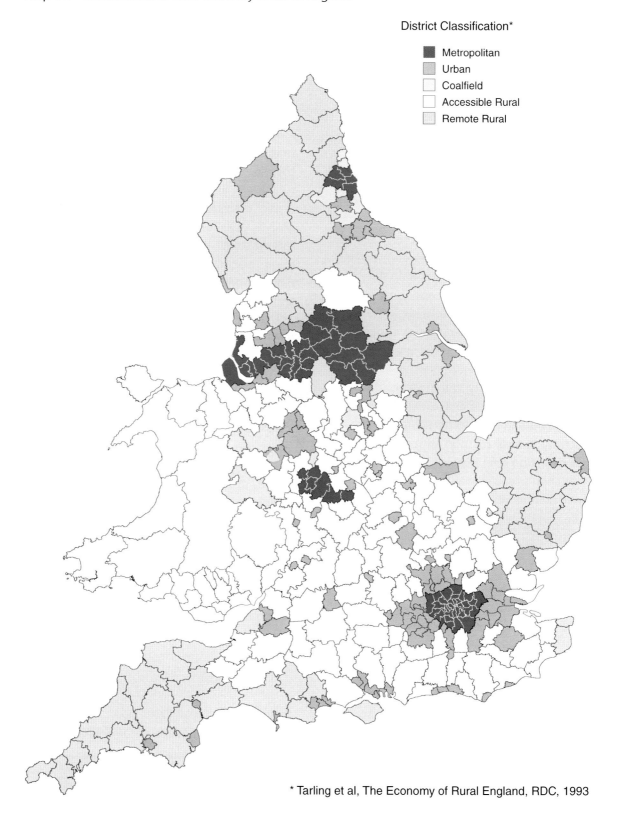

District Classification*

- ■ Metropolitan
- ■ Urban
- □ Coalfield
- □ Accessible Rural
- ▨ Remote Rural

* Tarling et al, The Economy of Rural England, RDC, 1993

Source: Rural Development Commission (Tarling et al) (1993), *The Economy of Rural England*

The diversity of rural economies

3.8   Current academic research suggests that there is, in fact, no single 'rural problem' that captures the diversity of social, environmental and economic challenges for people living and working in rural areas. Given the enormous range of landscape and settlement patterns in England, and the important effects of features such as road and rail links and proximity to major urban centres, this is no surprise. Further, this diversity is being fuelled by a marked shift in the distribution of the English population in recent decades which has transformed much of rural England. On aggregate, rural areas have been gaining population at a faster rate than other areas as people have moved from larger towns and cities. Linked to population growth has been employment growth and development pressures. However, this process of 'counterurbanisation' has been geographically uneven, and is producing new types of rural problems in different types of localities.

3.9   In some parts of the country, 'traditional' rural problems – economic and demographic decline and an over-dependent on primary economic activities – are of great significance. These problems are not confined to the former mining communities and to more peripheral areas such as the uplands: they are also to be found in parts of, say, rural Norfolk.

3.10   Other parts of rural England face difficult problems, resulting from rising levels of population and economic activity that combine to create tensions over further physical and economic development. New, and often more mobile and affluent, social groups move to rural areas which are seen as more attractive places to live and (sometimes) to work. The politics of preservation become hotly contested as struggles centre on defending those things (community, landscape, tranquility) which make them attractive. It should not be assumed, however, that rural areas facing this second type of problem are necessarily universally prosperous. For some more marginalised social groups within these areas, the processes and outcomes of social exclusion become hidden behind a dominant image of affluence and contentment. This has been the case in many of the more accessible rural areas that have gained population rapidly. The 'rural disadvantaged' become trapped within a world of mobility and affluence, as local economic, infrastructure and administrative networks are restructured around the needs of the mobile and affluent. Population growth in a local rural area can, for example, still be accompanied by a decline in local rural services.

3.11   There is an overall national geography to these two broad categories of rural problems; but in many regions and countries, the two can exist side by side. In short, rural England is experiencing a complex and diverse process of change that defies simple, uniform descriptions.

Urban and rural economies – similarities and differences

3.12   So, even using commonly accepted definitions and classifications, the differences among rural areas are arguably as great as the differences between urban and rural areas. But while it is difficult to make generalisations, some broad statements about the similarities and differences between urban and rural economies would be accepted by most commentators.

3.13 The *similarities* between urban and rural economies encompass:–

- Expert opinion and published data indicate that in most parts of the country there is a strong interrelationship (and hence interdependence) between economic activity in rural and urban areas – both in terms of trade and labour flows.

- There is a broad similarity between urban and rural areas in terms of the pattern of employment by economic sector.

- Urban and rural economies are increasingly being seen by national and local interests in a regional context – with new institutions such as the Regional Development Agencies being charged with responsibility for the economic development of the whole of their regions, rather than any geographical sub-set.

- Specific urban policies have an impact in rural areas, as where the regeneration of inner cities reduces the pressure for city-dwellers to move to the country

- Urban and rural economies are both subject to wider forces of globalisation and technological change.

- For both urban and rural economies, policies with a national sweep (whether instituted by national government or the EU) have a much greater impact on economic health than any specific urban or rural-tailored initiatives. As a means of influencing economic activity, even the most generously funded regeneration programme will run a poor second compared with the impact of the key macro-economic variables (in particular, interest and exchange rates), key fiscal measures (notably, rates of tax and duty borne by businesses) and overall expenditure policies for the main public services (health, education, and social security). That is why the best economic policy for any business – wherever it is

located – is the one that promotes macro-economic stability and creates the conditions for sustainable long-term growth. And it is why any recommendations made in this report are of secondary importance to what emerges from the Government's overall economic strategy.

3.14 Taken together, these similarities call into question some of the implicit assumptions behind traditional thinking on rural economic issues – in particular, the beliefs that a) there is a single rural economy, b) this is separate from the urban economy, and c) rural economic activity is fundamentally different from that in urban areas.

3.15 The *differences* between urban and rural economies include:–

- Agriculture and other primary industries (forestry, fishing, mining and aggregates) constitute a larger proportion – in terms of employment or GDP – of rural economies but nevertheless still represent only a minority of all employment in these areas.

- Open land is more plentiful in rural areas and its use – principally for farming, forestry and other land-based industries – creates not merely primary products but also a series of landscapes and habitats with associated environmental and aesthetic benefits.

- Most rural areas are characterised by a relative sparsity of population and distance from urban centres – and both of these features combine to create challenges for cost-effective service provision and the functioning of markets.

- There are fewer large (both in terms of workforce size and turnover) employers in rural areas and more micro-businesses (ie less than 10 people employed) and self-employment. Over 90% of employed people in rural areas are either self-employed or employed in micro-businesses.

Rural economies – strengths and weaknesses

3.16 As with the comparison between urban and rural economies, it is difficult to make generalisations about economic strengths and weaknesses across all rural areas. But to a greater or lesser extent, some of the physical and social aspects of rurality do give rise to sources of advantage and disadvantage for rural economies.

3.17 Rural areas have a number of *strengths* which underpin their economic performance:

a) They are perceived by many as offering a high *quality of life* for those who live and work there, as well as for those who visit. These quality-of-life benefits can be grouped under three headings:

- the physical environment – space, appearance of the landscape (and associated environmental public goods, such as wildlife and habitat), low levels of air and noise pollution, species diversity;

- the social environment – a different pace of life, a sense of community, a sense of safety;

- the quality of certain services – for example, primary education.

b) Underpinning these quality-of-life benefits, rural areas contain a wealth of *environmental, social and cultural resources* that can be harnessed for a wide range of economic activities – for example, tourism, recreation, countryside sports, equestrian activities etc.

c) They have a set of *potential competitive advantages* over urban areas for a narrower range of economic activities – for example:

- proximity to the natural resources (eg land) necessary for primary products and certain services (eg the recreation sector);

- lower costs (of labour and land, for example);

- greenfield sites;

- scope for expansion for economic development.

3.18 Two of the features that make rural areas attractive (and provide some of the sources of competitive advantage) – sparsity and limited physical development – also act as sources of *weakness* for economic performance:

a) Population sparsity, when allied to limited transport infrastructure, limits the size of labour markets in rural areas: this can create both shortages of skilled labour and underemployed or over-qualified workers unable or unwilling to travel.

b) A sparse population and dispersed settlement pattern also leads to practical difficulties in the cost-effective provision of support services (both public and private) for businesses in rural areas: for example, the decline in the number of banking outlets in rural areas in recent years.

c) These difficulties extend to the provision of infrastructure more generally – so facilities such as fibre-optic cable and ISDN telephone lines are comparatively rare in rural England, because the high fixed cost of infrastructure installation is not justified by the low levels of use from the sparse population.

d) Finally, sparsity inhibits the growth of broad, informal networks among entrepreneurs and managers – networks which, according to social-capital theorists such as Robert Putnam, underpin economic dynamism by creating opportunities for trading, collaborating and learning.

Rural economies – key facts and performance data

3.19 Box 3A provides an overview of some of the key facts and figures that highlight the nature of England's rural economies. These points are explored in more detail in Chapter 5.

Box 3A: Rural economies – a snapshot of key data[2]

Demographic Structure

- Up to a quarter of the English population lives in rural districts.

- The population in rural districts grew faster (24%) than in England as a whole (6%) over the last 25 years (1971 – 1996).

- People in rural areas tend to be older than in the rest of the country: 18% of the rural population is aged over 65 years compared with 16% nationally[3].

Economic Structure

- Some 29% of the English labour force works in rural districts.[4]

- Employment growth in rural areas has been faster than urban areas.

- Unemployment in rural districts is generally lower than average (4.2% for rural districts and 6.1% across England), but there is significant variation between areas, with some areas well above the national average.

- The mix of industrial sectors in rural areas is similar to urban areas – the main difference is agriculture, which accounts for 4% of employment in rural areas and less than 1.5% in urban areas.

- There is variation within rural areas, however, and agricultural employment can be as high as 20% in some rural districts.

- 8 out of the 10 counties with the lowest GDP per capita are rural.[5]

- Agriculture's share of national income has fallen from 2.9% in 1970 to 1.0% in 1998.

Rural Environment

- Rural districts account for 82% of the total land-mass of England.

- Over half the national population would like to live in rural areas because of the perceived quality of life they offer.

- The rural environment is under threat from economic development and agricultural intensification:

  - in 1993, 53km^2 of rural land – an area the size of Oxford – was developed (41% of all land developed in England);

  - one third of all hedgerows in England were lost between 1984 and 1993 (and these losses follow dramatic losses over the 1960s and 1970s).

Social Conditions

- Despite low unemployment, poverty exists in rural areas; though levels are slightly lower in rural areas (30% of the population) than urban areas (40%).

- DETR studies show poverty in rural areas can be a persistent problem.

- More people in rural areas rely on private transport – usually cars.

[2] The economic, environmental and social trends in rural England are explored in more detail in Chapter 5

[3] ONS (1996), *Mid-year Population Estimates*

[4] NOMIS (Aug 1998), *Labour Force Survey*

[5] Countryside Agency (1999), *State of the Countryside*

4. FROM HERE TO MODERNITY – THE CHANGING FRAMEWORK FOR RURAL POLICY

Summary

Post-war rural policy put security of food production centre-stage. Environmental concerns centred, by and large, on preventing urban sprawl. This policy framework contributed to the spectacular growth in agricultural productivity and output in the post-war period and managed the increase in the proportion of land used for housing.

But the values, beliefs and behaviour on which post-war policy was based have not proved to be permanent. Social and economic trends have, over time, combined to produce a fundamental change in views about what the countryside is for and in priorities for public policy.

There have been incremental changes in policy, but much of the policy framework developed immediately after the Second World War remains largely intact. In short, there is a mismatch between the needs of today's countryside and traditional patterns of policy-making.

Government policy for rural economies – the post-war framework

4.1   The current framework for rural policy has its roots in the early post-war period and, in particular, in the 'twin pillars' of the Agriculture Act 1947 and Town & Country Planning Act 1947. These Acts, together with a series of Acts from the mid to late 1940s covering the provision of public services (in particular, education and health), have constituted the main foundations of domestic policy for rural areas from the time of the Attlee Government to the present day.

4.2   In the late 1940s, the food security fears of the Second World War and memories of the agricultural depression of the 1920s and 1930s were still uppermost in the minds of policy-makers – food rationing was not phased out until the 1950s, for example. The post-war framework therefore sought to encourage the expansion of domestic food production through the provision of guaranteed prices for farm commodities, production subsidies, special tax treatment for farmers, the protection of agricultural land, and the encouragement of agricultural modernisation through technological change.

4.3 Agriculture was treated as the primary economic function of rural areas and seen as the most important strategic sector of the rural economy. Wider rural development policies were pursued through the work of the Development Commission (latterly the Rural Development Commission), but these policies were small in scale, and given a secondary task to 'sweep up' the socio-economic problems that resulted from agricultural change.

4.4 Membership of the European Economic Community in 1973 required the UK's entry into the Common Agricultural Policy (CAP). Crucially, from this time on, any major change to the framework for agricultural policy in the UK would have to be agreed among the partner Member States as part of a Europe-wide policy – and other Members States' policy objectives and farm structure differed widely from those of the UK.

4.5 During the early part of the post-war period, the goals of agricultural policy were not seen as in conflict with countryside protection. Agriculture was widely regarded as a steward of the countryside, and pollution of air and water, for example, tended to be equated only with urban and industrial areas. Concerns to promote recreational activities in the countryside or the conservation of rural landscapes and habitats were secondary to the pursuit of agricultural productivity and tended to focus on agriculturally more marginal land in the uplands. The main problems facing rural areas were seen as problems of population decline, geographical peripherality and technological 'backwardness'. In addition, rural areas on the fringes of towns and cities were seen as under threat from urban sprawl and so were protected by Green Belt legislation.

4.6 In line with the policy priority of ensuring sufficiency and security of food supply, the planning system afforded special treatment to the agricultural sector. An agricultural land use classification system graded land according to its agricultural productivity and placed a presumption against the development of more productive agricultural land. Farm buildings were also exempted from development control.

4.7 Financial support for the agricultural sector was also seen as a means of tackling rural poverty. Public services in rural areas were planned on the basis of universal provision, although local authorities did carry out some key settlement planning to rationalise service provision on a more cost-effective basis.

The successes of the post-war period

4.8 Rural policy in the post-war period had a number of key foundations. It was based on a clear vision of what rural areas – and their economies – were for, and on a clear set of values and priorities that reflected public concerns. The policy framework reflected, supported and reinforced these assumptions. This combination of clarity and consistency brought significant benefits – principally in the performance of the UK agricultural industry and in the consequent supply of food for UK consumers, but also in the protection of parts of the English countryside.

4.9 This framework, combined with economic and technological developments, brought about immense change in the agriculture industry, allowing substantial and sustained growth in productivity and output. This growth, allied to the development of trade patterns between the UK, Europe and the rest of the world, allowed domestic concerns about the security of food supply to be addressed. Moreover, the transformation of agriculture also brought significant improvements in food safety and quality. These improvements included: the elimination of TB infection via milk; the management of previously widespread animal diseases, such as brucellosis; the introduction of animal breeding programmes to help farmers produce lean meat, in response to nutritional advice and consumer demand; and the development of plant breeding that increased yields and resistance to disease.

4.10 Similarly, the Acts of the late 1940s proved successful in preserving aspects of the landscape and the environment in designated parts of rural England – for example, National Parks. Anxieties about the inexorable encroachment, US-style, of cities into adjacent countryside have not been borne out. And key areas in rural England have been protected from excessive physical development that could have destroyed their character.

Change in the countryside

4.11 But the values, beliefs and behaviours on which the post-war framework was based have not proved to be permanent:–

- As the issues surrounding security of food supply have been addressed and disposable incomes have risen, public concern about food has shifted from quantity to quality – with a much greater focus on issues of choice, convenience and safety. Indeed, the success of post-war policy in expanding food production has provoked public concern about over-production and its financial, economic and environmental consequences.

- Rising affluence and changing tastes have led to a reduced emphasis on the countryside as a resource for production and a greater emphasis on its potential for 'consumption', both as a place in which to live and in which to enjoy leisure and recreational opportunities.

- Partly as a reaction to the problems of doing business in cities and partly because of the increasing desirability for many people of living in the countryside, a growing consensus has emerged that rural areas are appropriate for more than just land-based activities (so a wider range of manufacturing and service businesses have located in rural areas).

- There has been a marked increase in levels of interest and concern for the environment and also a broadening of what the environment is perceived to comprise (e.g. to include biodiversity as well as air and water quality).

- More people see themselves as having a stake in the countryside (and in particular, in the state of its environment): and the views of rural residents have diversified, reflecting the changing social composition of the rural population.

- Partly as a result of greater mobility but also because of broader social trends, there has been a weakening of ties to local communities – with the result that many of the traditional self-support systems embedded in community networks have been eroded.

- Demand for higher quality services – along with a reluctance to pay higher prices and taxes for private and public services – has placed pressure on the extensive networks of service provision that existed in the 1940s and 1950s, with closure of many outlets in areas of dispersed settlement.

4.12 These trends impact on different parts of rural England in different ways. But, taken together, they amount to a fundamental change in views of what the countryside is for and in principles and priorities for public policy on rural issues, as well as in the pattern of social and economic life in rural areas.

4.13 Since the 1970s successive governments and the European Community have made a series of incremental reforms to the policy framework, in part as an attempt to reflect these changes in beliefs and behaviour but also to respond to growing concern about – and criticism of – the policy framework. The costs of public support to the agricultural sector, coupled with the costs of storing and disposing of agricultural surpluses helped fuel a critique of the framework. In other words, there was growing evidence that the existing policy framework itself was creating or worsening problems such as habitat loss, overproduction and excessive spending on subsidies. Another stimulus was the accumulating evidence that improvements in agricultural productivity were being achieved at the expense of the quality of the rural environment. Since the 1970s, a proliferation of studies has revealed the scale and extent of loss of valued landscape features such as woodland and hedgerows on agricultural land, as well as the loss of the wildlife that depended upon these habitats. Landscape rationalisation had been fuelled by the system of price support that rewarded farmers for increasing the scale of production.

4.14 Public concern became more acute in the 1980s and early 1990s, as policies of intensification began to have consequences for the safety of the environment and of agricultural produce. Between 1979 and 1988, for example, the number of farm pollution incidents more than doubled[1]. And the late 1980s were host to two major crises of food quality and safety – salmonella in eggs, and the BSE epidemic.

4.15 Increasing concerns about the environmental implications of agricultural techniques, along with the rising costs of agricultural support, began to prompt calls for fundamental reform of agricultural policy.

In response, the UK began to develop agri-environmental policies (designed to limit the worst effects of agricultural intensification in particularly attractive or valuable local agricultural environments) during the 1980s; subsequently, these became the model for the European schemes. There has also been a considerable growth in legislation to protect and enhance the environment, with the EU playing a leading role.

4.16 Pressure has not been confined to the agricultural components of the post-war framework. Many of England's more rural areas have been gaining population at a faster rate than other areas and have experienced a net increase in population of 24% between 1971 and 1996 as people have moved out from larger towns and cities. Population growth has been linked to employment growth and development pressures. These processes of social change in rural areas have helped produce new types of political pressures and conflicts at the local level over how the countryside should best be managed.

4.17 These pressures for change have accelerated at a time when the policy framework has become significantly more Europeanised. As a result, a large proportion of the change to rural policy in Britain has been driven by European-wide processes of policy reform. The Europeanisation of rural policy has brought both procedural innovations and substantive changes. For example, the expansion of the EU Structural Funds since 1988 has delivered significant new resources and procedures for the development of Integrated Rural Development Programmes in particularly fragile rural regions (under the Objective 5b programmes and the LEADER Community Initiative). These programmes have imported innovative systems of partnership, co-financing, strategic planning and

---

[1] NRA (1992), *Influence of agriculture on the quality of natural waters in England and Wales*, Bristol NRA.

community participation into rural development policy in England.

4.18 The European programmes represent an important first step in establishing a more 'joined up' and integrated approach to rural development with a territorial, rather than a narrowly sectoral, focus. Substantial resources have been put into these programmes. By the mid-1990s, EU rural development schemes totaled around £70million per year in England, equivalent to four times the amount usually distributed by the former Rural Development Commission for regeneration. A breakdown of the various spending programmes for agriculture and rural development is contained in Table 4.1.

4.19 The most significant European policy for rural areas is the Common Agricultural Policy – a combination of financial support and market regulation aimed at supporting

Table 4.1 – Programmes for Rural Areas in England 1999–2000

Rural Programme	Annual resources (£)
Agriculture, Fisheries and Food (estimated, using 1998/99 figures)	3 135
Of which:	
compensation payments	*1 265*
agri-environment	*110*
support for less favoured areas	*28*
Objective 5b (estimate)	63
Countryside Agency	42.9
English Nature	44.7
National Park & Broads Authorities (England & Wales)	19.3
(Note: the £19.3m refers only to the grant from central government. The Park authorities also receive income from local government, the EU, other grants, and self-generated income. Their total expenditure in 1997/98 was £48.2 million.)	
Regional Development Agencies (estimated)	
– ex-Rural Development Commission regeneration; and	20.4
– ex-English Partnerships regional regeneration	23.2
Single Regeneration Budget (estimated)	50
Housing Corporation (Rural housing programme)	17
Rural Transport Fund	51.7
National Forest Company	3.1
Regional Selective Assistance (estimated)	30
National lottery awards (all distributing bodies, 1998/99)	208

Sources: MAFF (1999), *Departmental Report*; DETR (1999), *Annual Report*; DTI (1999), *Annual Report*; Association of National Park Authorities (1997/98), *Annual Review*; HMT (1999), *Public Expenditure Statistical Analyses 1999/2000*; DTZ Pieda (June 1999), Public expenditure in Rural Areas, draft report for Countryside Agency; *National Lottery awards website* (www.lottery.culture.gov.uk); PIU estimates.

the European agricultural industry. The CAP has been incrementally reformed, particularly since the mid-1980s, initially in response to pressures arising from chronic food surpluses and the consequent budgetary costs of storing and disposing of them. Milk quotas were introduced in 1984, followed by the agreement of agricultural budgetary guidelines in 1988. Subsequently, in response to growing international pressures for the liberalisation of agricultural trade and the reduction of those subsidies coupled to farm production, a wider package of change – the so-called MacSharry reforms – was agreed in 1992. These reforms reduced some support prices, introduced direct income compensation for those cuts, and developed further the concept of a European rural policy in the form of accompanying social and agri-environmental measures.

4.20 The 1995 Uruguay Round Agricultural Agreement brought agriculture under the ambit of the GATT, and a new round of World Trade Organisation talks on agricultural trade is due to commence at the end of 1999. The previous Uruguay round included a 'Peace Deal' that prevented challenge of the CAP, but this deal expires in 2003. The trend is for the progressive reduction of tariffs and market support. In response to these looming international trade pressures, and to those pressures on CAP finances generated by the prospect of EU enlargement to the East, the European Commission published proposals (under the banner of 'Agenda 2000') in 1997 for further CAP reform. The proposals extended the 1992 reforms with a set of further price cuts, covering a wider range of agricultural sectors, and the introduction of a significantly greater degree of subsidiarity for Member States in implementing parts of the CAP.

4.21 The reform package was agreed at the Berlin Summit in March 1999, but the reductions in support prices were less than

originally had been proposed, and a proposal to reduce compensation payments over time (termed 'degressivity') was not accepted. However, the Berlin reforms are a significant further step in the process of CAP reform. They also include the rationalisation of several accompanying social, agri-environmental and structural measures into the new Rural Development Regulation (RDR) – the 'Second Pillar' of the CAP. Over the longer term, it is the Commission's intention that as price support and compensation payment subsidies are further reduced, so some of the savings can be redirected to wider rural development and environmental supports in rural areas through the RDR.

4.22 Across the 15 members of the EU, the approach to rural development policy is increasingly being conceptualised and developed in the context of regional development. This is reflected, for example, in the expansion of resources given over to rural development in the Structural Funds between 1988 and 1999, as well as in the changing division of responsibility between various Directorates-General of the European Commission. In England, this trend has gained impetus since 1997 as a result of the Government's approach to regional development issues and the remit of the new Regional Development Agencies for the development of the whole of their regions.

A mismatch between values, priorities and policies

4.23 There have been a number of beneficial changes to policy since the 1970s. Environmental practice is more tightly regulated; levels of price support for agriculture have been reduced; and the Government has developed policy tools for supporting more environmentally friendly practice among farmers. But in spite of these incremental changes, much of the policy framework developed immediately after the

Second World War remains largely intact; and a number of the key components of the framework from the late 1940s still drive Government action today.

4.24 In contrast to the Whitehall of the 1940s where a number of industries enjoyed dedicated ministries, MAFF is now unique among government departments in devoting the majority of its efforts to intervention in a single industry – agriculture. That industry still experiences different treatment in terms of planning, taxation, and production support. The planning system remains better equipped for yesterday's problems of rural depopulation and urban sprawl than for the more complex problems of what has been called the 'contested countryside' in the late 1990s. And the debate about service provision remains couched in the language of universality and uniformity, even though the social problems in rural areas require more flexible, tailored solutions that take advantage of technological and social trends unimagined by Whitehall policy-makers in the late 1940s.

4.25 In short, there is a mismatch between an emerging new paradigm for rural issues and a policy framework still shaped by the concerns of the early post-war period. To assess the impact of this mismatch, it is necessary to examine more closely the trends, opportunities and threats facing rural economies – the subject of the next chapter.

5. RURAL ECONOMIES: TAKING STOCK – TRENDS, OPPORTUNITIES AND THREATS

Summary

Rural England has seen a structural shift in economic activity away from primary industries to service sectors over the past two decades (though more slowly in agriculture, due mainly to subsidies). Most rural economies have coped well with the need for structural economic adjustment. Employment levels in rural areas are higher than in urban areas and have been growing faster than in the economy as a whole. But some rural areas still face barriers to economic dynamism associated with sparsity and remoteness, or an over-dependence on declining industries.

The quality of the rural environment is a source of economic advantage to rural areas and is greatly valued by the public. But aspects of the rural environment are under threat as a result of the development pressures generated by population movements from urban to rural areas, and the continued influence of the CAP upon farming practices.

Social exclusion exists in rural areas and can be harder to tackle because the individuals concerned are geographically dispersed. The number of service outlets in rural areas has declined, jeopardising access to services for less mobile and socially excluded people.

Access to transport is extremely important in rural areas, but public transport is unlikely to be able to meet all the needs of rural dwellers.

5.1   Chapter 4 has outlined the shifting post-war consensus about the role of rural economies. The purpose of this Chapter is to set out the main changes that have taken place in rural economies over recent years and to consider likely future trends given unchanged policies. It includes:

- a review of the main *economic* changes that have taken place, focusing in particular on the role of agriculture;

- a review of the main changes in the rural *environment* and the forces behind them;

- a review of the main social trends covering both problems of *social* exclusion and service provision.

Economic trends

5.2 The past 20-30 years have seen significant economic changes in rural economies. Using employment data[1] as a measure of the structure of rural economies, the key trends over the past 15 years (1981 –1996) have been:

- a decline in agricultural employment in rural areas from 6% to 4% of total rural employment;

- a decline in employment in other primary industries (e.g. coal-mining) from 2.5% to 1%;

- an increase in employment in the service sectors from 60% to 71%.

5.3 Table 5.1 gives more detail of the breakdown of rural employment by industry within these sectors.[2]

Manufacturing and service sectors

5.4 Overall, rural England appears to have coped well with the need for structural economic change. Employment in rural areas has increased more rapidly than in other

Table 5.1 Employment in rural areas, 1996 – by sector[3]	
Primary industries	**9%**
Of which:	
Agriculture	*4%*
Energy & water	*1%*
Construction	*4%*
Manufacturing	**20%**
Of which:	
Food& beverages	*3%*
Textiles, apparel & leather	*1%*
Wood, paper & other	*4%*
Chemicals, rubber, plastic, etc	*3%*
Metal & machinery	*8%*
Services	**71%**
Of which:	
Distribution, hotels and restaurants	*24%*
Transport and communications	*5%*
Banking, finance, insurance etc	*13%*
Public administration, education & health	*24%*
Other services	*5%*

Source: NOMIS (1996), *Annual Census of Employment.*

[1] NOMIS (1981), *Small Area Statistics*, (1996), *Annual Census of Employment.*

[2] NOMIS (1996), *Annual Census of Employment.*

[3] The figures for employment understate the contribution of agriculture, as agriculture has a much greater degree of self-employment. Self-employment accounts for 12% of those working (employed or self-employed) in England, and accounts for a third of those working in agriculture.

Map 5.1 Percentage of People in Employment (England Only)

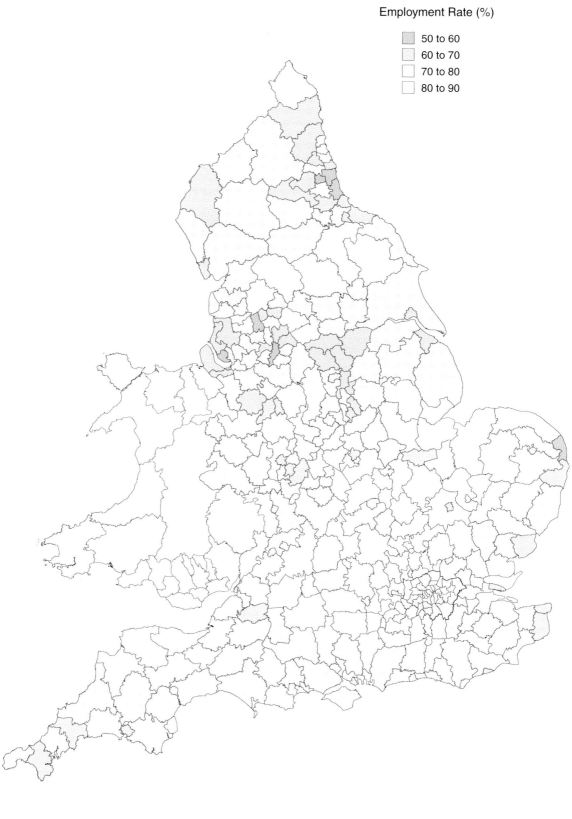

Employment Rate (%)

50 to 60
60 to 70
70 to 80
80 to 90

Source: *Labour Force Survey, April 1998*

Chart 5.1: Employment Change by Sector 1991 – 1996

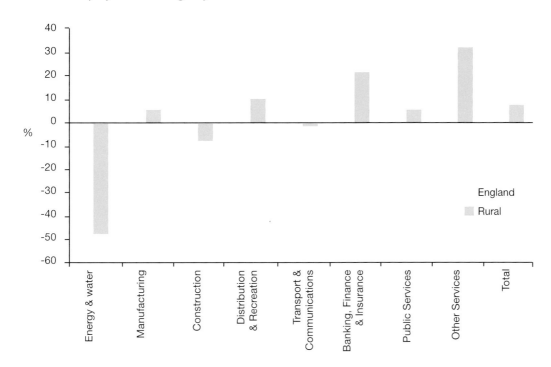

Source: *Countryside* Agency (1999), *State of the Countryside.*

areas of the country over the past 10 years (see Chart 5.1). Map 5.1 shows the variation in employment levels, and the higher than average levels in accessible rural areas. And *unemployment* in rural areas is generally lower than in the rest of the country (4.2% for rural districts compared to 6.1% in England in 1998)[4].

5.5   There are a high proportion of micro businesses in rural areas, with over 90% of all rural firms (including self-employed and those below the VAT threshold) employing less than 10 people. Research by the Rural Development Commission[5] suggests large firms (employing over 100 people) are less common in rural than in urban areas (at 1.4% of rural firms compared to 2.2% of urban firms).

5.6   There is evidence too that in the late 1980s and early 1990s rural businesses were more dynamic than their urban counterparts. Over the period 1979–1990, the number of

VAT registered businesses increased by 25%. This masked a differential between urban and rural areas, with growth in rural businesses reaching 27% compared to an increase in urban areas of 23%. By 1997, some 42.5% of the VAT-registered businesses in England were located in rural districts.

5.7   The higher rate of small firm formation in rural areas appears in part to be the result of the perceived quality of life in rural areas. Almost two-thirds of rural firms are set up by people who have moved into the area compared to one-third of new urban firms (Table 5.2). Three-quarters of those who moved to rural areas stated that the environment was of 'some' or 'great' importance in the decision.[6]

5.8   Within this largely positive overall picture, however, some rural sectors and rural areas have experienced problems. Employment in primary industries other than

[4]   *Labour Force Survey* (August 1998).

[5]   RDC Research Report 37 (1998) *Larger Firms and the Rural Economy.*

[6]   Keeble, Tyler, Brown and Lewis, (1992) *Business Success in the Countryside*, Department of the Environment.

Table 5.2 Origins of Entrepreneurs setting up new firms			
	Remote rural	**Accessible rural**	**Urban**
Born in area	42.4	34.2	65.6
Moved to area before setting up firm	36.5	52.5	25.9
Moved to set up firm	21.1	13.3	8.6
Total	**100.0**	**100.0**	**100.0**

Source: Keeble, Tyler, Brown and Lewis (1992), *Business Success in the Countryside*, Department of the Environment.

agriculture has declined more steeply than in farming. In coal mining and other areas dependent on mineral extraction industries, the decline in employment has been particularly severe. From 1960 to 1995 the number of people employed in coal-mining fell from 583,000 to just over 10,000, with the number of deep mines falling from 698 to just a handful.[7] This has resulted in higher levels of unemployment in many mining areas – which, in some cases, has persisted for decades.

5.9   More generally, areas affected by the rapid decline in primary industries have found it difficult to adjust. It has not been easy to develop alternative sources of employment in areas where one industry once dominated. This challenge has been exacerbated by the areas' remoteness, sparsity of population and poor transport access.

5.10 There are parts of rural England, therefore, where unemployment levels remain high. Such areas tend to be remote and to have a high dependence on agriculture or another primary sector (such as mineral extraction). Map 5.2 shows the pattern of unemployment in rural England.[8]

Agriculture

5.11 These trends in employment necessarily give only a partial picture of what has been happening to agriculture. A fuller analysis of the circumstances of the industry needs to explore the trends in output, productivity, government expenditure and farming income.

5.12 In terms of output, the decline of agriculture has been relative to other industries rather than absolute. Total agricultural output has risen in real terms but not as fast as in other industries. Chart 5.2 shows how, for the UK as a whole, agricultural output has fallen as a proportion of national income. By 1998 agriculture accounted for only 1% of national income compared with 3% in 1973.[9]

5.13 There are significant variations in the importance of agriculture to rural economies in different parts of the country. Chart 5.3 illustrates the regional variation in agricultural output as a proportion of national income in different regions of England. Agriculture is of greater importance in East Anglia and the South West (though there is no region where the industry accounts for more than 5% of GDP).

[7] NOMIS (1995), *Annual Census of Employment.*

[8] *Labour Force Survey*, (March – May 1998).

[9] MAFF (1999), *Agriculture in the UK, 1998.*

Map 5.2 Percentage of People out of work and claiming benefits in Rural Areas (England Only)

Claimant Rate (%)

7.5 to 10
5 to 7.5
2.5 to 5
0.5 to 2.5

Source: *Labour Force Survey, April 1998*

Chart 5.2: Agriculture – share of national income and value of output

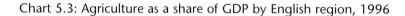

Source: ONS, UK National Accounts (GDP at current factor cost, by industry).

Chart 5.3: Agriculture as a share of GDP by English region, 1996

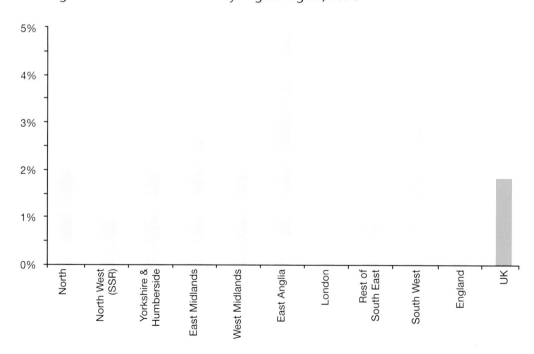

Source: ONS, (1998), *Regional Trends.*

Similarly, although agriculture is declining in importance overall, there are still areas where it is a very significant employer. Map 5.3 shows those areas where employment from agriculture is greater than 10%.

5.14 Agriculture has achieved sustained improvements in labour and total productivity (see Chart 5.4), which helps to explain why employment has declined even though real output has increased.

Map 5.3 Percentage of Workforce Employed in Agriculture (England Only)
by Local Authority District, 1997

% of Workforce

25 to 30
20 to 25
15 to 20
10 to 15

Source: MAFF estimates

Chart 5.4: Trends in Agricultural productivity in the UK

Source: MAFF (1999), Aggregate Agricultural Account.

These improvements have been linked to a process of restructuring that has removed many smaller-scale producers from the industry. The average farm size in the UK is considerably higher than the rest of the EU.[10]

5.15 Agriculture receives significant public support, currently some £5 billion per annum in the UK, of which over £3 billion goes to England, through the Common Agricultural Policy (CAP), Structural Funds and domestic programmes. Notwithstanding the 1992 CAP reforms, which sought to reduce the full

economic costs of state support for the industry, public expenditure on agriculture has increased substantially in recent years – (see Table 5.3 below). This increase is in part because the reforms shifted support from indirect subsidies (through price support) to direct subsidies (through compensation payments) – though it is also because of the financial impact of BSE.

5.16 CAP support in terms of direct payments is unevenly distributed around the country, as shown by Map 5.4, and is skewed away from

Table 5.3 – UK expenditure on agriculture since 1992 (nominal)	
Year	Total Managed Expenditure: agriculture, fisheries, food and forestry (£million)
1993/94	4,112
1994/95	3,655
1995/96	4,119
1996/97	5,979 (incl 1,496 BSE related expenditure)
1997/98	5,012 (incl 954 BSE related expenditure)
1998/99	5,017 (incl 579 BSE related expenditure)

Source: HM Treasury (1999), *Public Expenditure Statistical Analysis.*

[10] European Commission DG6 (1999), *Rural Developments – CAP 2000 Working Document*, Brussels.

Map 5.4 CAP Direct Payments to Farmers (English Counties): Average expenditure per
Agricultural Hectare, 1997

Average Spend per Hectare (£)

- Above 250
- 200 to 250
- 150 to 200
- Below 150

Source: MAFF

the geographically peripheral rural areas and concentrated in eastern England.

5.17 Farmers have faced particular difficulties since the mid-1990s, notwithstanding efforts to diversify into non-farm activities. The long-term changes in UK agriculture have been overlaid in recent years by the BSE crisis. Also, after benefiting from exchange rate moves in the early 1990s, farm incomes dropped back when Sterling appreciated against other European currencies in 1996 and 1997. As a result of this combination of cyclical, structural and external fiscal factors, farm incomes have declined sharply since 1995[11] (though these lean years were preceded by a marked rise in farm incomes earlier in the decade, following the UK's exit from the European Exchange Rate Mechanism). Chart 5.5 shows the trend in UK farm incomes over the past twenty-five years.[12] It is important to note that the "farm income" measure used to summarise the financial health of UK agriculture does not correspond to the income or "take-home pay" of farmers themselves. It is closer in concept to a measure of business profitability.[13] In consequence farm incomes might be expected to fluctuate as profits do in other sectors.

5.18 Within the overall picture of economic difficulties, some agricultural sectors are doing better than others. (Charts 5.6 & 5.7) show the relative performance of various sectors in terms of net farm income (taking 1991 as the base year).

5.19 Farmers have looked increasingly for new sources of income to supplement agriculture. There has been a significant trend towards diversification into tourism and other recreation-based activities, agri-businesses or non-agricultural activities.

Chart 5.5: Trends in Total Income from Farming, income per head and direct subsidies in the UK (real terms, 1998 prices)

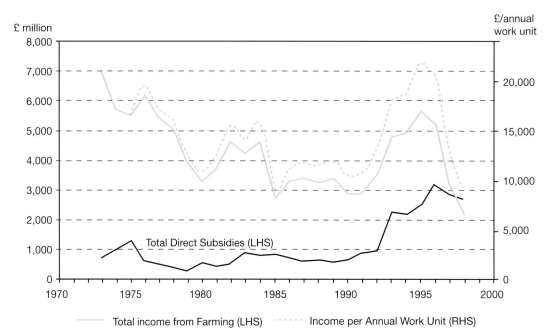

Source: MAFF (1999), *Agenda 2000 CAP Reform: A new direction for Agriculture*; HM Treasury.

[11] MAFF (1998), *Trends in Total Income from Farming*

[12] MAFF (1998), *Trends in Total Income from Farming*

[13] Total income from farming = business profits plus income to those with an entrepreneurial interest (farmers, partners, directors, their spouses and most family members) – source: MAFF (1999), Farm Incomes in the UK 1997/98

Chart 5.6: Net Farm Income by Sector (1991 as Index)

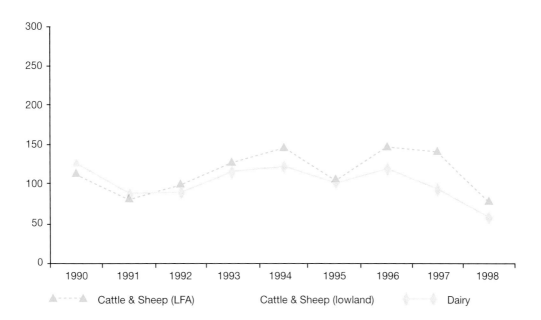

Source: MAFF (1999) *Farm Incomes in the UK, 1997/98.*

Chart 5.7: Net Farm Income by Sector (1991 as Index)

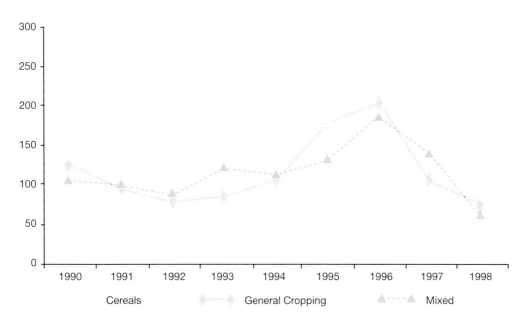

Source: MAFF (1999) *Farm Incomes in the UK, 1997/98.*

Average net income generated 'off-farm' in 1997/8 was £5,000 (including social security payments and pensions) compared with average net income of £16,266 from all sources. Nearly two-thirds of farms receive some off-farm income.[14]

Environmental trends

5.20 The quality of the rural environment is one of the most important factors in the appeal of rural areas as places in which existing inhabitants are happy to live and

[14] MAFF (1999), *Farm Incomes in the UK, 1997/98.*

stay – and places to which many city-dwellers would like to move. Some 89% of people living in rural areas say they are content with where they live, compared with less than 20% of people in cities.[15] A recent Gallup poll found that 71% of people believed the quality of life is better in the countryside than elsewhere and 66% said they would move to the countryside if there were no obstacles to doing so. However, widespread appreciation of the quality of the countryside is matched by a widespread concern that it is under threat. For example, DETR's survey of 'Public Attitudes to the Environment' found that nearly half the respondents were concerned about the use of insecticides and fertilisers and the loss of plants and animals.[16] In 1997, some 91% of respondents in a poll for the Countryside Commission agreed that "society has a moral duty to protect the countryside for future generations".

5.21 The quality of the environment in many rural areas has come under pressure from two fundamental forces in recent decades:

a) *the shift of population from urban to rural areas*

5.22 Between 1971 and 1996 the Census of Population shows an increase of 24% in the population of rural England, compared to 6% across England as a whole (see Chart 5.8). Research by Champion[17] estimates that in 1990/91 there was a net movement of 80,000 people from urban to rural (or mixed urban/rural) areas. Between 1981 and 1991 there were an average 77,000 in-migrants to England's rural districts per year.[18] This reflects the attractiveness of rural environments but creates increasing demand for housing in rural areas and pressure for new roads, infrastructure and the development of services to support the increased population.

Chart 5.8: Rural and urban population growth

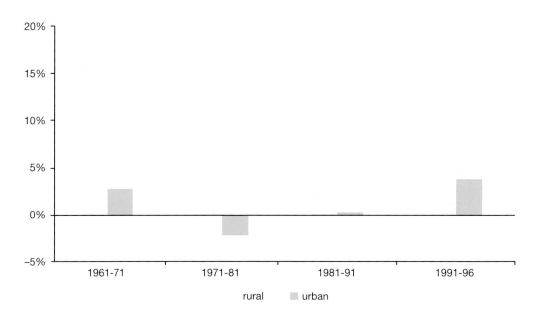

Source: Census of Population, OPCS Population censuses.

[15] Countryside Commission (1997), *Public Attitudes to the Countryside, 1997.*
[16] DETR (1998), *Digest of Environmental Statistics.*
[17] A. Champion et al. (1998) *Urban Exodus*, London: CPRE.
[18] RDC (1998), *Household Growth in Rural Areas.*

5.23 As a consequence of these population shifts:

- an area of grassland the size of Bedfordshire was developed between 1992 and 1997 in the UK (122,000ha).[19]

- some 44% of sites that were developed between 1983 and 1993 were in rural districts (although only 25% of the population lives in rural districts).[20]

- There is a recognition by Government that many of the estimated 3.8m homes necessary by 2021 will have to be built on greenfield sites, though the Government aims to restrict this greenfield development to a maximum of 40% of new housing units.

b) *the impact of the Common Agricultural Policy*

5.24 The other main driver has been the CAP which, through production support, has encouraged the intensification of farming. Intensification has involved mechanisation, the use of pesticides and the partial or total removal of features such as stone walls and hedgerows in many rural areas. Agriculture is intimately linked to the environment in rural areas since it accounts for 85% of the land area of rural England and 75% of the land area of the whole country.[21]

5.25 Of course, not all agricultural development has been unfavourable to the rural environment. Organisations such as the Farming and Wildlife Advisory Group and local environmental action groups are strenuous in their attempts to improve the environmental quality of rural areas, and there are many schemes, some Government-funded, that aim

to improve the environment and seek to offset or reverse environmental damage. However, the overall trends remain a cause for concern: the quality of the rural environment has shown some deterioration on a range of indicators over recent decades, as shown below:

- between 1984 and 1994 1/3 of hedgerows were lost (158,000km) through general deterioration or replacement with fences.[22]

- only half of all dry stone walls were considered to be in good or secure but deteriorating condition in 1994.[23]

- wild bird populations have declined by more than 10% since 1970.[24] Numbers of farmland birds such as the tree sparrow and the grey partridge have declined by 87% and 78% respectively since 1970.[25]

- in 1997/8 only 55% of SSSIs were in favourable condition (i.e. their environment was being well-managed and was not deteriorating), and 12% were in a poor state and declining.[26]

- Damaging activities occurred on 69 SSSIs in 1997/8 (an area of 7,182 ha, compared with 3,262 ha in 1996/7). Some 88% of the land damaged in 1997/8 was as a result of agricultural activities – usually over-grazing of uplands, the effects of which can normally be reversed by reducing stocking levels.[27]

5.26 It is disturbing trends such as these which have led the Government to offer more protection to hedgerows, dry stone walls and Sites of Special Scientific Interest (SSSIs). The Government has also proposed a series of indicators of sustainable

---

[19] CPRE, Press Release 1999.

[20] DETR (1998), *Land Use Change in England no. 13.*

[21] DOE (1990), *Countryside Survey.*

[22] Institute of Terrestrial Ecology (1994), *Hedgerow Survey.*

[23] Countryside Commission (1996), *The Condition of England's Dry Stone Walls.*

[24] DETR (1998), *Sustainability Counts: headline indicators.*

[25] DETR (1999), *Sustainability Indicators.*

[26] English Nature (1997/98), *Annual Report.*

[27] English Nature (1997/98), *Annual Report.*

development. These are both important initiatives: the first in addressing existing problems, the second in measuring their effectiveness and providing information on future trends which could pose a threat to the environment or the landscape.

Social trends

5.27 Poverty in rural areas is a significant and persistent problem, though less prevalent than in urban areas (Chart 5.9). The proximity of affluent and deprived households in rural areas makes it harder (and more time-consuming[28])

to identify social exclusion in statistical data. Definitions of poverty vary, and studies exploring the incidence of rural poverty tend to vary in their estimates.[29] However, all agree that poverty in rural areas exists, and that a sizeable proportion of the population is affected.

5.28 A recent report by Chapman, Shucksmith and colleagues on poverty in rural areas[30] based on a sample of 5,000 household incomes suggested that 30% of individuals in rural Britain had experienced poverty in the last decade, compared with 40% in urban areas. Studies into rural

Chart 5.9: Income distributions in urban and rural areas

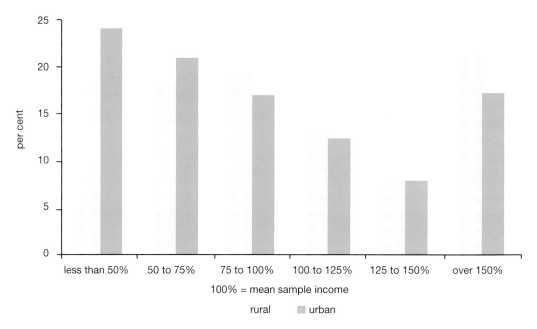

100% = mean sample income

rural   urban

Source: Chapman et al (1998), *Poverty and Exclusion in Rural Britain,* Joseph Rowntree Foundation.

Box 5A: Social Exclusion in Rural Wiltshire

A 1998 study into poverty and social exclusion in Wiltshire found that 40% of households in one village had an annual income of over £40,000 and a further 40% had incomes of under £8,000. This was despite a very low local unemployment rate (2.4% compared with the national average of 6.2%).[31] While this study may not be indicative of all rural communities it illustrates the point that poverty in rural areas often exists alongside affluence.

[28] P. Milbourne et al. (1998) *Disadvantage in Rural Hampshire*, Cheltenham & Gloucester College of Higher Education.

[29] RDC (1998), *Rural Disadvantage – Understanding the Process.*

[30] P. Chapman et al (1998), *"Poverty and Exclusion in Rural Britain"*, Joseph Rowntree Foundation.

[31] P. Milbourne et al (1998), *Poverty and Social Exclusion in Wiltshire*, Cheltenham & Gloucester College of Higher Education.

poverty in the 1970s[32] and the 1990s[33] for DETR found that 25% of households in rural areas were living in, or on the margins of, poverty. Box 5A describes the income polarisation that can occur in rural areas.

5.29 The greater number of people retiring to rural areas and low wages are the main contributors to rural poverty, according to the RDC.[34] Poverty in rural areas is not restricted to remote regions – it can be found in accessible and seemingly affluent places.

5.30 However, the rural population is healthier than that in urban areas, with lower average standardised mortality rates (SMR) which may suggest the quality of life partly compensates for lower incomes (see chart 5.10). The SMR in rural areas in England is 94: for urban areas, it is 101 (and the average for England is 98).[35] In short, even after taking account of differences in age and

sex of their populations, people in rural areas live longer – though coalfield areas, with their relatively high mortality rates, are an exception to this rule.

Service provision

5.31 A range of sources confirms that the number of service outlets in rural areas has declined in recent years, threatening to increase the exclusion of people without access to transport. The most extensive source, in terms of scope and ability to track trends over time, is the RDC's database of periodic surveys of rural services. The PIU has drawn on the 1997 RDC survey of the 9,677 rural parishes in England,[36] which can be compared with their 1991 survey. In addition, the National Federation of Women's Institutes' 1998 survey[37] of the 8,000 WIs in England and Wales, 83% of which are

Chart 5.10: Standardised mortality rates, UK = 100

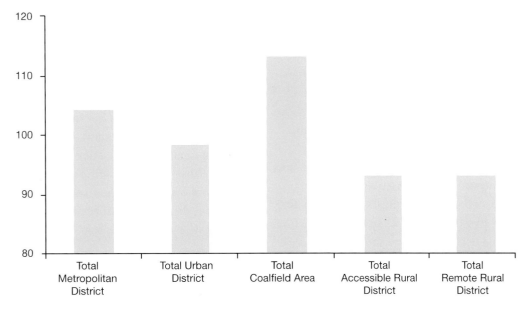

Source: ONS.

[32] McLaughlin (1986), *The Rhetoric and the Reality of Rural Deprivation* Journal of Rural Studies, Vol. 2, 291–307.

[33] P Cloke et al (1994), *Lifestyles in Rural England*, Rural Development Commission.

[34] RDC (1996), Disadvantage in Rural Areas.

[35] ONS (1998), Regional Trends.

[36] RDC (1997), *Survey of Rural Services.*

[37] National Federation of Women's Institutes (1999), *The Changing Village.*

considered rural, provides useful data. Finally, the PIU has drawn on the survey of Rural Community Councils contacted annually from 1996 to 1998.

5.32 These surveys can only be illustrative of trends because:

- they have differing methodologies and survey bases;

- the data is not from random samples (e.g. WI data may perhaps come from wealthier areas, there is some variation in number of responses to questions, and people are more likely to respond on issues of concern) and so may not be representative; and

- only limited comparisons over time are possible.

5.33 Trends for some key services are set out below:

- *Village Shops* – The RDC found a small reduction in the proportion of rural parishes had no shop (42% in 1997, compared to 41% in 1991). They suggested that closures were mainly in parishes with under 300 population or in larger parishes where there was more than one shop. The WI found that 30% of rural villages had no shop and 1,100 village shops had closed since 1988. The WI report also noted a marked reduction since 1988 in specialist shops such as butchers, bakers and greengrocers (which may also have happened in towns and cities). In 1996 and 1997 two-thirds of RCCs said that there had been a decline of village shops in their area.

- *Post Offices* – The Post Office reports that its rural network has shrunk from 9,700 in 1994 to 8,900 at present. The RDC found 57% of rural parishes in England has a post office. RCCs reported a steady decline in the number of rural post offices from 1996 to 1998.

- *Village halls* – The RDC found that 72% of rural parishes had a village hall or community centre in 1997, an increase from 70% in 1991, and very few parishes had no meeting place, as there were usually alternatives such as church or school halls. The WI reported that 90% of villages had a village hall or community centre, compared with 46% in 1950. This increase reflects funding that has been available for village halls since the 1930s, most recently from the RDC and the Millennium Commission.

- *Other Services* – The RDC found that in 1997 49% of rural parishes had no school (for any age), 83% had no GP and 29% had no public house, although there was little recorded change in the levels of these services from 1991. However, in 1997 and 1998 RCCs were particularly concerned about pubs and the majority reported 3–5 closures in their area – particularly in less densely populated areas with no tourist trade. The RDC found that 91% of rural parishes had no bank or building society in 1997, compared with 89% in 1991.

5.34 Not all these trends should be taken as evidence of a decline in the quality of service provision. Often, the rationalisation of dispersed service outlets has led to an increase in quality: for example, in some forms of health and education provision. But for those residents with poor mobility, the loss of a service in their settlement is likely to reduce their quality of life – and to exacerbate problems of social exclusion.

Transport

5.35 Access to transport is extremely important in rural areas, and continually emerges as one, if not the main, issue for those living in rural areas. Concerns include:

- The general decline in public transport over a number of decades and until recently its continuing deterioration in at least some rural areas. This decline has a significant impact upon the old, young people and many women without access to a private car;

- Increases in public transport fares and the cost of fuel; and

- Growing economic and environmental costs from the increase in road traffic and congestion.

5.36 Some 78% of households in rural districts now have one or more cars (and for settlements below 3,000 inhabitants, 84% of households have at least one car) compared to the national figure of 69%. DETR projections suggest that the proportion of rural households with cars will rise from 78% to 85% by 2026.[38] However, it is car use which poses the greatest threat to the environment and to the quality of life in the countryside, rather than car ownership. The costs of using a car have hardly risen in real terms in recent years, while the costs of bus and rail have gone up considerably. This makes public transport less and less viable, and undermines its frequency and reliability. Partly as a result, road traffic has been growing faster in rural areas than others and projections show this trend continuing, which will result in increased congestion and environmental costs.

5.37 The Government's integrated transport strategy, by investing in more and better quality public transport to provide greater choice, seeks to encourage car owners to use public transport when they can. Car tax has been reduced for less polluting cars, bringing the cost of ownership down, while rises in fuel duty have helped to narrow the gap between private and public transport.

5.38 The 1997 RDC survey suggests that public transport services have declined over the last decade, with the number of rural parishes without any bus service increasing from 14% to 22% between 1991 and 1997. Rural parishes with daily services (at least 5 days a week) fell from 67% to 66% of parishes over this period.[39] The recent WI report (see footnote 37) suggests a similar loss of services. However, National Transport Survey data suggests that, overall, rural households have better bus services now than in 1985/86. This may reflect a trend for bus services in more populated rural areas to improve and for some contraction in more sparsely populated areas. The extra money announced in the Government's 1998 and 1999 Budgets for rural transport has led to a significant increase in rural bus services. Initial data on usage presents a mixed picture, as might be expected; there are some success stories alongside other services with low usage (although patronage will often take time to build up). Public transport fares have increased significantly above inflation.

5.39 Access to transport is vital for people in rural areas. Given the complex and dispersed journey patterns of many rural dwellers, private transport is often the only available option. Despite the Government's increases in fuel duty, at the national level motoring costs have remained fairly constant as a proportion of household income.

5.40 In addition, the link between transport and combating social exclusion in rural areas is important. Recent research for the Joseph Rowntree Foundation by Sarah Monk of Anglia Polytechnic University suggests that transport is a key problem for the rural unemployed in accessing jobs, while possession of a driving licence appears to be an important factor in moving off benefits.

Conclusion

5.41 This chapter has highlighted the principal social, economic and environmental trends that are currently unfolding in rural

---

[38] DETR (1997), *National Road Traffic Forecast.*

[39] RDC (1997), *Survey of Rural Services.*

England. Within this overall national picture of rapid and profound change, it is important to recognise the diversity of ways these trends may be experienced in rural areas, no two of which are the same. There can be no single, simple storyline that captures the full complexity of what is happening to England's rural economies, nor to the different social groups and businesses involved. What may be a threat for one group or locality could represent an opportunity for another. And even in a world where globalisation and technological changes are being said to erode distances and make geography less important, the challenges for England's rural economies will still depend, at least in part, on local socio-economic circumstances – such as local skill levels, labour markets, residential preferences and economic diversification strategies. But without a coherent framework of national policy, these challenges are unlikely to be met. The next Chapter outlines a policy framework that will allow an effective response to the diverse problems and opportunities of rural England.

6: MODERNISING THE POLICY FRAMEWORK

Summary

The post-war policy framework is in need of modernisation. New trends and developments have widened the mismatch between current policies and the real needs of the countryside. This mismatch contributes to some rural problems and prevents the resolution of others.

The new policy framework should be built around the vision of promoting and supporting productive, sustainable and inclusive rural economies. It should set objectives in the areas of: *economic policy*, where government needs to tackle failures in the market and improve its own interventions; *environmental policy*, where government needs the tools to sustain the environmental wealth of rural areas; *agricultural policy*, where the industry needs support to modernise and adapt; and *social policy*, where there is a need to forge a new commitment to rural communities.

The case for change

6.1　Many messages of importance to policy-makers emerge from the survey of trends, problems and opportunities outlined in Chapter 5. But perhaps the most important is that each of the key assumptions underpinning post-war policy has been superseded by new trends and developments:

- rural economies are no longer dominated by agriculture and other primary industries;

- the assumption that all farmers will act as benign stewards of the countryside, even when they face incentives to do otherwise, has been undermined by environmental damage arising from intensive farming;

- new concerns have emerged in relation to the environmental agenda;

- predictions of rural depopulation have been replaced by development pressures in much of rural England;

- universal provision of public services in, or close to, all settlements (through extensive networks of post offices, libraries, schools, cottage hospitals etc) has proved unaffordable – and in some cases has been shown to be ineffective;

- the belief that universal service provision and employment opportunities from primary industries would eradicate poverty and social exclusion in rural areas has not been borne out by events – these phenomena have persisted in rural communities, even through periods of relative prosperity.

6.2 Yet, as argued in Chapter 4, much of the policy framework developed immediately after the Second World War remains largely intact. Admittedly, the failure of policy to predict the future accurately is not unique to rural affairs; and the fact that a policy is based on an out-of-date assumption is not always sufficient reason for overhauling it. But the mismatch between the old policy framework and today's countryside is not a harmless inconsistency. It contributes to some problems and prevents the resolution of others; and it leaves the Government inadequately equipped to respond to the new issues and challenges. For example:

- policies on agriculture lead to poor use of scarce public funds and the sub-optimal allocation of national resources, create barriers to economic adjustment, and fail to ensure sufficient provision of environmental public goods;

- the concentration of policy-makers on agriculture in rural areas has led to a neglect of broader and more integrated strategies and policies for rural development – even though, given the shift of employment and output away from primary industries, these broader strategies and policies are necessary for effective government action in rural economies;

- planning policies can place limits on economic dynamism and diversification which do nothing to enhance the environment or landscape or of ensuring sustainable development;

- service delivery policies fail to join up the efforts and resources of different government organisations and to facilitate commercial and voluntary provision, with the consequence that many of the social and economic problems experienced by rural communities remain unaddressed; and

- while the Government has a large armoury of devices to assist policy-making and intervention, not all of these devices are effective or appropriate for rural settings and the Government still lacks key tools – in terms of data, performance measures and fiscal instruments – with which to understand and respond to trends and problems in rural areas.

6.3 In short, the post-war framework is in urgent need of modernisation. Without change, the Government will be at best a spectator as rural businesses and rural communities struggle to tackle the difficulties they face; and, at worst, it will be part of the problem. The Government needs a new policy framework that will allow it to respond effectively to the needs, problems and opportunities in rural areas today rather than those of 50 years ago.

6.4 In developing a new policy framework, the Government will need to be mindful of the opportunities and constraints that membership of the European Union and international bodies such as the World Trade Organisation brings. Many aspects of policy – notably in relation to agriculture, but also in relation to environmental and economic issues – are determined in Europe. This reflects the fact that many of the issues which face the countryside – such as agricultural subsidies, product standards and pollution – cross national boundaries. But it would be wrong to conclude that there is nothing within the UK Government's direct control: within the economic, environmental and social realms there are UK-specific policies and resource-allocation decisions that can be changed – and there are increasing opportunities for national flexibility with European frameworks.

The respective roles of government and the market

6.5   The new framework for rural policy must incorporate the lessons from recent decades about the limits and possibilities for government action and intervention in economic affairs. There is an emerging consensus among policy-makers about what works – and what does not. This consensus can provide a sound rationale for government action and allow the identification of principles that should shape and govern the activities of the state in the economy. (Note: the economic rationale for intervention, and the principles that should influence government action, are explored in more detail in Annex A3.)

6.6   Traditionally, government intervention is justified in terms of addressing market failures and/or distributional objectives.

6.7   *Market failures* occur when private transactions between agents in the market fail to produce the best outcome for society as a whole. This may be because:

- the goods are valued but have no market (public goods)[1];

- there are wider costs or benefits to society associated with the good or its production which are not reflected in its market price (externalities);

- one or more agents have imperfect information about the nature of the good;

- imperfections in the market mean that structural economic adjustment is excessively slow.

6.8   Governments' *distributional objectives* are ultimately a matter of political judgement, and may involve a trade-off with economic efficiency and growth. For rural England, these objectives have included tackling concerns about the equity between rural and urban areas, and about poverty and social exclusion (wherever the poor and socially excluded live).

6.9   There are a variety of initiatives that the Government can use to address the different forms of market failure and its distributional objectives. For example:

- act as the "provider of last resort" for public goods, for example through the National Parks and Forestry Commission;

- use and enforce legislation to protect and preserve public goods, for example through SSSIs and listed buildings;

- encourage and facilitate private provision of public goods, for example by the National Trust;

- reflect the wider costs and benefits to society of an activity in its price, through taxes and subsidies;

- help markets to price wider costs and benefits to society of an activity, for example through a system of tradeable quotas or permits;

- provide and facilitate access to information and advice;

- provide a regulatory safety net, for example maintaining health, safety and product-quality standards and addressing market power and abuse;

- build the capacity of communities to help themselves, with government, whether central, regional or local, playing a partnership role;

- use taxation and public spending to redistribute income.

---

[1]   In practice, there is no clear dividing line separating goods that are wholly private and those that are exclusively public. There are many goods that, while privately owned and provided, have some characteristics of public goods – for example, many landscapes. Importantly, some of these goods are not non-rival: i.e. there is an optimum level of consumption beyond which an increase in the number of consumers leads to falling levels of satisfaction. These goods are often termed 'club goods'.

6.10 With all of these measures, it is important to recognise the limits to government's role, the costs that intervention imposes (e.g. the burdens of regulation and taxes) and the fact that governments, as well as markets, can fail. These insights have driven efforts to improve the quality of regulation and encouraged a focus on the enabling role of government, rather than direct intervention.

6.11 Finally it is important to remember that discouraging or preventing people from doing something negative is not the same as encouraging them to do something positive. While tax and regulation may be successful in achieving the former, government also needs to use incentives to encourage positive behaviour. For example, regulation may be appropriate as a means of preventing farmers from removing hedgerows, but it is likely that some form of payment would be necessary to get farmers to reinstate hedgerows that no longer exist.

6.12 These insights into economic policy-making must influence the development of the new policy framework. But government cannot operate by economic insight alone. The new arrangements must be derived not only from economic theory but also from an analysis of rural problems and opportunities and a clear vision for rural England. The key rural problems that the new framework will need to address are outlined in Chapter 5. They include:

- the continuing high levels of public expenditure on agriculture;

- the competitive future of the agriculture industry;

- the process of structural adjustment out of primary industries – and the difficulties experienced by some rural areas in managing this adjustment quickly and smoothly;

- the barriers to economic dynamism in other sectors of rural economies;

- the threats to the quality of the rural environment;

- the persistent problems of poverty and exclusion in rural areas; and

- the difficulties of securing access to services and transport.

A vision for rural England and rural economies

6.13 The final ingredient for the new framework is vision – a sense of what rural economies should look like in the medium to long-term. As noted in Chapter 4, the post-war policy framework was informed and supported by a clear vision of what the countryside was for and a sense of the direction in which rural areas should be developed – and, for a number of years, this framework commanded a broad consensus. The old framework has become outdated, and the elements of a new one – based around new approaches to the rural environment, a different view of agriculture, greater economic diversity, the desirability of access and the need to sustain inclusive communities in rural areas – are starting to emerge. A new vision is needed, which incorporates and reflects these elements and which is capable of generating a coherent and effective set of policies that will allow its implementation.

6.14 Any credible vision should start from the recognition that the countryside is one of England's most valuable assets. It is a source of beauty, prosperity and well-being. And, perhaps most importantly, it is a source of environmental and historical resources that, if managed properly, can help sustain the existence of our society and of a diversity of species within nature. These insights are reflected in the Government's overall vision for the countryside[2], which has five strands:

a) a belief in a living countryside;

b) a belief in a working countryside;

c) a recognition of the interdependence of town and country;

d) a commitment to protect the rural environment and enhance its qualities;

e) a belief that the countryside should be accessible to all.

6.15 Economic activity is central to the realisation of this vision. Strong, vibrant rural economies underpin the things people value in the countryside: namely, rural communities and the rural environment. But rural economies also contribute to the wealth of the nation, especially in the production of goods and services for which they have a natural advantage – for example, in agriculture (and it is important to place continuing emphasis on the countryside as a resource base for food production), as well as in other forms of primary production and in certain types of tourism.

6.16 Strong rural economies can be created only by individuals and the companies and organisations in which they work. But the Government can play an important role in helping to develop and maintain such economies, both through its overall economic policies and through policies that address the specific problems and take advantage of the specific opportunities in rural areas.

6.17 The Government's overall economic aim is to raise the rate of sustainable growth and achieve rising prosperity through creating economic and employment opportunities for all. A number of the Government's economic objectives concern the economy as a whole and therefore apply to the economies of rural areas as much as those of urban areas. These general objectives are:

- to create a macroeconomic environment in which enterprise and wealth creation can flourish;

- to boost competitiveness and productivity;

- to ensure that economic development is sustainable;

- to improve the quality and cost-effectiveness of public services;

- to tackle poverty and social exclusion.

---

[2] DETR (1999), *Rural England – a discussion document.*

A new policy framework: the aim and objectives for rural economies

6.18 Given the different characteristics and problems of rural economies, it is unlikely that reliance on the Government's national economic objectives alone will be sufficient as a guide for makers of rural policy. Within the framework of these overall economic objectives there is a need for a further set of objectives that address the particular issues in rural areas, as outlined in the chapters above.

Overall aim

To encourage and support the creation of productive, sustainable and inclusive rural economies.

Objectives

1. To facilitate the development of dynamic and competitive rural economies – in particular, through:

   a) tackling the market and government failures that hamper rural economies;

   b) encouraging the operation of market forces in the agriculture sector, tempered by action to ensure good and safe practice and the supply of public goods.

2. To ensure that economic dynamism is environmentally sustainable (in part through pursuing the objective for the agriculture sector, outlined at 1b above).

3. To ensure more equitable access to economic & social opportunities in rural areas.

6.19 Each of the three objectives warrants some amplification:

- Objective 1 is concerned with economic issues, and is focused on tackling the causes of the economic problems highlighted in Chapter 7 of this report. The objective reflects the current consensus that the market represents the most efficient means of allocating scarce resources and therefore that governments should take steps to remove inappropriate and unjustifiable barriers to the operation of the market. Many of these steps apply to all sectors of rural economies; but the government faces particular challenges when developing policy for the agriculture sector, given the history of extensive intervention by government in agriculture and the consequent barriers to market mechanisms. By definition, dynamic rural economies will experience rapid change. This objective is concerned with helping rural areas to thrive on change. And it is also designed to ensure that, in this process of change, the productivity and competitiveness of the UK's agriculture sector is increased while upholding high environmental standards. The objective will be achieved through a wide range of measures, including those which address the market and government failures that cause problems in rural areas.

- Objective 2 is concerned with environmental issues, and is focused on ensuring that economic dynamism does not destroy the stock of environmental goods – the principal source of competitive advantage for rural economies. The objective will be achieved by developing processes and instruments (including regulation, taxes and spending programmes) that allow the integration of economic and environmental policies or the striking of balances and trade-offs where the policies conflict.

- Objective 3 is concerned with distributional issues: how to ensure that key services (both public and private) are accessible to everyone in rural areas who needs them – and how to do this cost-effectively, given the challenges created by sparsity and isolation. Since there is a limit to how far national taxpayers would be prepared to subsidise services in rural areas, the objective will be achieved by thinking creatively about how access to services can be improved (through the provision of transport or the use of new technologies), by looking for innovative ways to join up different elements of public and private provision, and by targeting services and resources to rural individuals in greatest need in order to tackle problems of rural poverty and exclusion.

Rural economies in 2010

6.20 One useful check on the appropriateness of the recommended objectives is to attempt a description of the results that they are likely to generate in the medium-term. It seems reasonable to assume that, with these objectives driving policy, the rural economies of 10 years' hence will have the following features and characteristics:

6.21 *An enterprising countryside:* Government policy and market dynamism will combine to stimulate enterprise, wealth generation and growth in rural England – providing economic strength and security for communities in the countryside, and strengthening the capacity to adjust to further structural change. There will be:

- a reduced burden of regulation on rural businesses;

- an enrichment of the skills base of rural economies;

- improved infrastructure in rural areas;

- improved provision of advice and support services for rural businesses; and

- improved support for the tourism and recreation sectors.

6.22 *A high-quality, well-managed environment:* England's rural environment will remain a source of beauty, wealth and pride – with more resources and greater protection for what we value most in the English countryside. There will be:

- a rise in the level of environmentally friendly practice across the agriculture industry;

- protection for the land of greatest environmental value from inappropriate development;

- greater opportunities for everyone to enjoy the countryside;

- improved land-use planning in rural areas, with more open and better informed debates at the start of the planning process about the needs of an area and how to balance economic and environmental objectives – debates that will engage the whole of a local community; and

- stronger mechanisms to limit and compensate for any damage to the rural environment caused by development.

6.23 *A sustainable agriculture:* England will enjoy an agricultural industry that can compete, survive and thrive in the 21st century – with farmers becoming rural entrepreneurs who can diversify their businesses to reflect market demand and their sources of commercial advantage. There will be:

- a reduced dependence of farmers on production subsidies, with a commensurate reduction in government expenditure;

- an increased level of support for farmers' contribution to the environment;

- a move towards a level playing field for agriculture and other sectors of rural economies;

- a reduction in red tape and an improved range of business advice and support services for farmers, making it easier to diversify and develop farm businesses;

- a continuation of the process of restructuring, creating more efficient farms;

- an improved relationship between farmers and their customers – so that farmers provide more of what the public wants in the way the public wants it; and

- a programme of more extensive reform within the EU, which the UK will have played a central role in shaping and driving.

6.24 *Thriving and inclusive communities:* Rural England will retain living, working communities – avoiding decline into commuter dormitories or museum villages – with improved access to services and resources. There will be:

- stronger rural economies, providing opportunities for wealth-creation and employment that are necessary for the vitality of rural communities;

- improved access to public, community and commercial transport services;

- improved access to public and private services in rural areas – with public bodies encouraged to pool resources and make greater use of mobile provision, and through new ways of harnessing the power of new technologies to overcome problems of distance and sparsity;

- more effective targeting of services to address social and economic problems;

- continuing provision of social housing in rural areas as part of a commitment to sustaining balanced communities; and

- a strengthening of many market towns as centres of economic activity and service delivery.

6.25 Underpinning this view of the future is the recognition that rural areas will be places of profound and significant change. This is not a new phenomenon: change has been a constant feature of rural economies – particularly the agricultural sector – over the past 50 years, as a consequence of national and European policies. Continuing change is inevitable, and often desirable (eg CAP reform). Not all change is likely to be comfortable and popular with everyone: but, guided by the aim and objectives outlined at para 4.18, it should be possible to manage the process of change to secure the best possible outcome for rural communities and for the nation.

The need for action now

6.26 Statements of vision and objectives are necessary for an effective response by government to the economic problems and opportunities of rural areas and to what people want and need from rural areas; but they are not sufficient. The new framework must be supported by a set of policies, processes and instruments that give practical effect to the objectives, shifting the focus from 'where do we want to go?' to 'how do we get there?' The objectives generate a need for action in four main areas:

- *economic policy* – to support an enterprising countryside;

- *environmental policy* – sustain the environmental wealth of rural areas;

- *agricultural policy* – to develop a competitive, forward-looking, modernised industry; and

- *social policy* – be to forge a new commitment to rural communities.

The following chapters address each of these imperatives in turn.

7. ENCOURAGING AN ENTERPRISING COUNTRYSIDE

Summary

Dynamic and competitive rural economies are not only compatible with strong rural communities, and proper protection for the landscape and environment. Without strong economies, adapting to change, the future for many rural areas would be difficult, and the environment and landscape would suffer too. The Government has two duties: encouraging economic growth and prosperity; and intervening where the market alone is not enough, or could be positively harmful.

Government should look at ways to improve the skills and employability of those who live and work in the countryside, at the infrastructure in the countryside, particularly in fast-moving areas such as telecommunications, and also at the support available to help businesses start up and prosper.

Government must also change and improve the ways it intervenes, casting aside outdated assumptions and find better ways of shaping and influencing the development of rural economies. Support for key sectors such as tourism, culture and recreation could be more proactive. Intervention in areas such as agricultural regulation and land-use planning may need to be recast.

Introduction

7.1   If it is to implement the new objectives on rural economies successfully, the Government will need to steer a course between taking the wrong action and taking no action. Neither post-war interventionism (with an emphasis on government control, subsidies and attempts to 'pick winners'), nor the laissez-faire approach which assumes that the market solves all problems, will work. Instead, the Government should have positive policies for the problems that it can and should do something about, but otherwise stops distorting and restricting the decisions of individual economic agents. Five areas need to be looked at:

- the skills base of rural economies;

- the infrastructure of rural areas;

- the provision of advice and support services for rural businesses;

- support for the tourism and recreation sectors;

- government regulation of rural economies.

The skills base of rural economies

7.2.   Though many rural areas have highly skilled and productive workforces, rural economies face difficulties. Some areas and groups have clear skills gaps. Training provision does not always match needs, and needs are not always understood at a regional and local level. Smaller firms (which predominate in rural areas) face the greatest difficulty in funding training and in releasing staff for external training. Sparsity is a problem too: many businesses are too thinly spread to form effective traditional networks of support, and they and their staff are often far away from training outlets. Government has a clear role to play in helping to overcome these difficulties.

Skills gaps

7.3   Overall, rural areas have skill levels at roughly the average for England. Some 39% of the workforce in rural areas have NVQ Level 3 or above (the equivalent of two or more A levels) compared to 37% of the workforce in urban areas.[1] However, this picture masks two problems: below-average levels of marketable skills in remote rural areas; and a less entrepreneurial approach among some farmers compared to other rural business people.

7.4   The first problem is in part due to skilled workers having the wrong skills. The most pressing problem is skilled workers who need training and reskilling as part of the process of structural adjustment. There will also be a continuing need in the short to

medium-term for training those workers displaced from agricultural employment, as restructuring continues to reduce the size of the agricultural workforce.

7.5   The problem of less entrepreneurial behaviour among some farmers may be a legacy of the heavily interventionist frameworks that have dominated agriculture throughout the post-war period. Government has not encouraged farmers to see themselves as rural entrepreneurs. As market forces become more significant in agriculture, so the farming industry will need to become more skilled at understanding and responding to the needs of customer segments, managing supply chains, innovating and adapting rapidly to changing market conditions, and watching and learning from (and often collaborating with) competitors.

Training need and provision

7.6   With the move from 73 TECs to 47 Learning and Skills Councils, there is an opportunity to reappraise the provision of training in rural areas. One option may be to give the regional tier of the public sector (probably RDAs, in consultation with GROs and regional assemblies) an explicit responsibility to develop strategies and plans for skills development to meet the needs of rural areas within their regions as part of their regional skills action plans, influencing the work of the learning and skills councils and also of Lantra, the National Training Organisation for the land-based sector of the economy. Particular attention should be given to programmes that will help smooth structural adjustment. While much of the money needed to deliver these strategies is already within the system, some limited additional resources might be obtained from the EU by including a range of rural skills and

[1]   NOMIS (March – May 1998), *Labour Force Survey.*

vocational development initiatives within the English programme for the Rural Development Regulation.

7.7 The University for Industry (Ufl) provides a new opportunity to address the learning needs of rural areas (see Box 7A for more details). In particular, it will combat the problems of sparsity and distance that limit access to training opportunities in rural areas, where the nearest college is often still a long way away and may offer only a limited range of courses. There is also a particular focus on access to learning in the workplace, addressing the problems that small businesses (which predominate in rural areas) have in releasing staff for training. The Ufl will complement and build upon existing accreditation and information programmes – for example, Lantra's SkillCheck.

7.8 The Ufl could create a rural business school, using internet, multi-media and open learning technology. This could offer a rural MBA programme, supported by diploma and other shorter courses in specific fields – for example marketing and finance/accounting, as well as environment/ecology and other aspects of land management. In developing new courses such as the rural MBA, the Ufl should work in collaboration with institutions such as the Royal Agricultural College, and build on other existing initiatives. Such an initiative could help to address the skill needs of rural businesses, and help to create a wider support network for rural entrepreneurs in agriculture and other industries.

Infrastructure in rural areas

Communications

7.9 Internet-based activity is moving from being the exception to the mainstream in most sectors of the economy, even for small firms. Businesses which concentrate on digital activities are particularly suited to a rural environment. Indeed, given the ability of information and communications technology to liberate firms from the need to be in a particular geographical location, and the desirability of living in a high quality rural environment, the information sector could become a major source of growth for rural economies over the coming decades.

7.10 But the poor communications infrastructure in rural areas means that rural businesses are currently not well placed to take advantage of this. ISDN technology currently limits this service to users within three miles of a telephone exchange or sub-exchange – and, as these facilities tend to be located only in larger settlements, businesses in rural areas must make do with much slower Internet access. The problem is not confined to land-based telephony: at present,

Box 7A: The University for Industry

The University for Industry is at the heart of the Government's strategy for lifelong learning and will be launched in Autumn 2000. It will help adults of all ages and in all occupations learn everything from basic literacy to advanced business management, with a particular focus on overcoming the barriers to learning – time, cost, uncertainty, inadequate information, complexity, lack of confidence and inconvenience. The Ufl is intended to connect learners with high quality products, commissioning new learning packages to fill gaps, and taking full advantage of multimedia technology, open and distance learning, the National Grid for Learning and a network of Ufl Learning Centres across the country.

For further information, see: http://www.ufiltd.co.uk

none of the mobile-phone license-holders has managed to provide universal reception coverage across England. The percentage of land covered varies, with less densely populated and geographically peripheral rural areas more likely to miss out. The limitations of this coverage will become particularly acute over the next few years as third-generation mobile phone technology (allowing direct Internet access, and offering a means of overcoming the lack of land-based broader-band infrastructure) becomes more widespread.

7.11 There are limits to what the Government, usually acting through its telecommunications regulator, can do to overcome these problems. In many instances the financial and environmental costs are likely at present to outweigh the benefits. Given the current low levels of use of ISDN technology by businesses and homes, it would not be appropriate to enshrine access to ISDN as part of any Universal Service Obligation. And the current costs to the telephone operating companies (and eventually to customers) of installing land-based infrastructure to provide broader-band communications for all rural settlements might be prohibitively high. But two practical, smaller-scale steps can be taken to improve matters.

7.12 The first step is for regional and local government to obtain information from telephone operating companies about the extent of current and planned broader band coverage within their areas and use this information both to influence regional and local economic development and land-use planning policies and to assist companies with determining where they might locate.

7.13 The second step is for them to consider using regeneration and rural development resources to fund extensions of land-based and mobile telecommunications infrastructure – for example, through the installation of

leased lines into smaller settlements with a business base that would benefit from improved communications. The Government could, for example, consider including an element for funding these extensions within the Rural Development Regulation programme (as well as using additional EU resources for those areas benefiting from Objective 1 and 2 programmes).

Other infrastructure

7.14 Many rural areas lack the more basic infrastructure – transport links, business sites etc – that underpin economic activity. The high levels of initial expenditure required to build such infrastructure, along with the difficulties of using rents and charges to capture the full economic benefit once it is built, make individual companies reluctant to fund infrastructure developments. There is thus a case for government involvement – not just in granting the necessary planning approvals for new infrastructure but also in financing the initial investment that the market will not supply. As with any investment project, there are risks in government seeking to impose solutions from above, but these risks could be managed by concentrating on small-scale developments, working closely with local communities (see Box 7B).

7.15 EU money has been used effectively for this sort of project (for example, the LEADER programme has supported a series of local initiatives); and there may be further scope for using EU resources – perhaps from the Structural Funds or, in the longer-term, the Rural Development Regulation. But the Government should also look at ways to ensure flexibility in national policy and spending – particularly in relation to transport infrastructure – in balancing environmental, economic and social objectives. An example of this is set out in Box 7C.

Box 7B: Case Study – Ardglass Marina, Northern Ireland

Ardglass is one of four fishing-dependent villages on the East coast of Northern Ireland. The local community identified an unfulfilled tourism potential which was combined with a heavy reliance on fishing (experiencing long term decline). They put together a proposal under the Fishing Villages Programme for a sixty-six berth Marina (for recreational boats) and raised £50,000 from the local community (total cost was £1,600,000). LEADER, IFI (International Fund for Ireland) and the EU's Fishing Villages Programme (PESCA) funds made up the remainder. The marina separated the commercial and recreational fleet and provided many more recreational spaces than previously existed. The scheme also built a small administrative building containing a kitchen, showers and a small meeting room.

There was no tourist accommodation in the village before the marina opened and there are now 4 B&Bs and two restaurants. Local shops report turnover is up by 50%. Bookings for the marina are very strong (with 3,000 overnight stays by crews per annum), and the scheme made a £25,000 profit last year. The influx of overnight visitors to the community is estimated to have generated about £166,000 spending locally p.a.[2] The staff are all volunteers (effectively two full-time posts) who are strongly committed to the project.

The next phase of the community development includes a shop front restoration scheme and a proposed expansion of the range of services and facilities available. This would include water-based recreational activities (e.g. wind-surfing, canoeing), as well as accommodation and restaurant facilities (which will be used to generate profit to fund posts currently operated by volunteers).

Box 7C: Redevelopment of the former Markham Colliery site

The former Markham colliery site in Derbyshire is immediately adjacent to the M1 and could provide employment opportunities to former mining communities in the area, which has not adjusted successfully to the closure of the pits (in part because of the poor transport infrastructure in the area) and has continued to experience high levels of unemployment.

The redevelopment of the colliery is likely to be successful only if a new junction is installed on the M1 adjacent to the site ('Junction 29A'). This would be likely to have considerable costs, and also to have implications for traffic growth and for the environment. As for all projects of this kind, effective decision-making needs to balance the projected costs and potential environmental impact against the likely benefit to the local economy and the local community.

[2] Commercial Supplement, Irish Times, (1998).

Support and advice for rural businesses

7.16 The sparse distribution of businesses across rural areas means that they tend to be further away from both public and private sector service providers. It also means there are few other rural businesses nearby, limiting the scope for informal support networks. Small operators are less likely to be able to afford to market their business very effectively.

7.17 There are a number of ways in which government can help to overcome these problems – in particular, through the provision of advice and support, shared facilities (for example, ICT-equipped small business centres), and support for the development of rural business networks. This should mean small rural firms in particular are offered help to form marketing co-operatives and take advantage of new information technology such as the internet to reach wider markets.

7.18 The new Small Business Service (SBS) should address some of the key criticisms leveled at its predecessor, the Business Links network. Business Links were intended to serve businesses with 10 or more employees. This excluded the vast majority of businesses in rural areas. In practice, many Business Links recognised this gap and provided small business advisors for these smaller firms. However, the focus on numbers of businesses advised – and the need to recover at least 25% of costs through fees – tended to skew Business Link activity away from rural and micro businesses.

7.19 The SBS is explicitly charged with addressing the needs of micro-businesses (0 to 9 employees), as well as those of larger small firms. The SBS will need to ensure that this is not compromised by its other objectives; and that its performance in rural areas is as effective as that in urban areas. To achieve the latter objective, the SBS should absorb and replicate the best practice of Business Links in rural areas – which included using peripatetic advisers and regular surgeries in rural centres. The SBS will need to ensure that its rationalised sub-regional structure (there will be 45 to 50 SBS franchises compared with 81 Business Links) does not result in an excessively urban focus. One way of checking on the SBS's performance might be to ask the Countryside Agency to include an assessment of the quality of advice and support for rural businesses in its annual report on the state of the countryside. This might cover the SBS's success in:

- maintaining sufficient focus on the needs of micro-businesses and absorbing the best practice of Business Links in rural areas;

- ensuring that the single gateway principle works in practice in rural areas;

- providing services to farms and other agricultural businesses; and

- encouraging local authorities to provide information on land-use planning and on the availability of sites and buildings for commercial purposes, and working with authorities to put farmers and rural landowners with redundant sites/buildings in touch with potential occupants.

7.20 In addition, the SBS will provide a single gateway to business advice and support – delivering many services itself and providing an entry-point to more specialised services provided by others. This offers an ideal opportunity to overcome the fragmented arrangements in rural economies where support and advice for farms (provided not by Business Links but by other organisations – in particular, ADAS) have usually been separate and distinct from support and advice for other rural businesses.

7.21 Some local authorities are piloting the use of registers of sites and buildings for commercial purposes, so that a business interested in locating within the authority's boundary can be informed of where they might go. Such registers also provide a useful opportunity for farmers and other rural landowners interested in converting their redundant buildings, by putting them in touch with potential occupants. The SBS should encourage local authorities to provide such services and integrate the resulting information into its work.

7.22 Although significant domestic resources have been set aside in national and local budgets for the provision of business advice, the opportunity exists to supplement these under the Rural Development Regulation. These funds could be used to grant-aid the development of shared facilities, business networks and mentoring schemes in rural areas, along the lines of existing good practice (see Box 7D).

Box 7D: Examples of support for rural businesses

Welsh Development Agency Mentoring Scheme – The scheme is a WDA/TEC partnership with ERDF funds, piloted in West Wales for small rural companies that are either on the verge of expansion or are of strategic importance to the area. The scheme initially funds an executive mentor to transfer skills and knowledge to build up expertise within the company that it currently lacks. The aim is for the company and the mentor to develop a long-term relationship that encourages the company to contribute to the costs and eventually enter into a direct agreement with the mentor for continuing support. Mentoring activity has covered a range of issues including strategic planning, managing growth, introducing new technology, securing funding, human resources and the environment.

The pilot scheme achieved a range of benefits including: improved turnover, enhanced business skills, development of new products, established links with other businesses, creation and safeguarding of jobs, and increased knowledge and take-up of other support schemes offered by the TEC, Agency and other organisations. The companies' views were that the main dividend was improved confidence, more focused on strategic issues, delegated more, managed a business not a product, and dealings with financial institutions were more structured.

The scheme is now expanding to provide support for SMEs throughout the rest of Wales.

Dumfries and Galloway Rural Business Ring – The Local Authority is co-ordinating the process of establishing a rural business ring in partnership with the Small Business Federation, Forestry Commission, Scottish National Heritage, the Local Enterprise Company, local Agricultural Colleges and the Scottish National Farmers Union.

The aim is to provide a communications network for farming and other rural business/interests with a view to facilitating the passage of information, and creating benefit through increased knowledge and improved efficiency. The group aims to build on the organisations and working arrangements that are already in place to increase co-operation and encourage more joint-working arrangements on the supply, production, processing and marketing efforts of local businesses. The partnership is seeking funding to kick-start the process and intends to launch in September.

Support for the tourism and recreation sectors

7.23 Governments need to exercise caution in moving beyond broad measure to help all businesses of the kind outlined above to focus on any one sector. But there are sectors of rural economies – notably, tourism and recreation – where some additional forms of government action seem appropriate. Together, these sectors:

a) are of strong and growing economic significance: it is estimated that in 1997 rural tourism generated £12bn of consumer spending and supported – directly or indirectly – 380,000 jobs in rural areas;[3]

b) are well-suited to gaining jobs and wealth from the countryside without threatening its essential character: 81% of visitors to Britain said the quality of countryside and heritage had been important factors in their decision to visit;[4] and

c) help sustain local communities: seasonal tourist income can make the difference between profit and loss for local services such as buses and shops in rural areas and enable them to remain open for the benefit of local people as well as tourists.

7.24 Despite their economic significance, these sectors are prone to market failure. The small scale of most suppliers and the fragmented nature of the sector can lead to missing markets, with insufficient resources allocated to marketing . And as with any other kind of infrastructure, funding the facilities (such as long-distance trails or visitor information) needed for attract visitors can be hard. Individual firms may sometimes not be willing and able to finance such facilities, even though they would benefit from the extra business they would generate along with the wider local community.

7.25 While tourism makes a significant contribution to rural economies in aggregate, the benefits are unevenly distributed across England. Some rural areas are overwhelmed and suffer congestion and environmental degradation. Others fail to attract visitors, perhaps because of poor marketing or infrastructure. Already, many tourist and local authorities engage in joint marketing of facilities and publicity campaigns – both domestically and abroad – to promote less well known rural destinations in England. But there is a wider question of whether government – at central or local level – should take action to manage problems of tourist congestion more directly or to ensure that the full economic costs of tourism (including any damage to sites arising from excessive number of visitors) are captured. There are many options available to government, from placing restrictions on the numbers that can visit locations at peak times through to systems that use charges (whether voluntary or mandatory) to generate revenue for local environmental protection and enhancement. Charges that have been trialled in the UK and other countries fall into two main types:

a) *tick box schemes* which are voluntary charges operated in hotels and restaurants. Visitors literally place a tick in a box and pay an additional charge as a gesture of good will and as a conscious decision to contribute towards the infrastructure of the area they are visiting. A continental variant is a compulsory tourist tax levied at accommodation. The revenue generated can then be used to develop tourist infrastructure and to repair environmental damage.

b) *toll and car parking schemes* that are mandatory and aim to restrict the number of visitors to an area and can be integrated

---

[3] RDC (1997), *Economic Impact of Recreation and Tourism in the English Countryside.*

[4] English Tourist Board, Consumer Survey 1996.

with park and ride schemes. Such schemes raise practical issues around how to ensure the local population is not disadvantaged (i.e. local exemptions); how to operate such schemes where there are lots of small roads into an area (e.g. through a rural licensing scheme) and rights of access for those who cannot afford tolls. But, under certain circumstances, such schemes can play a valuable role in rationing access to over-crowded areas, as well as generating revenue which can be invested in local infrastructure and environmental schemes. Parking charges could be used in some areas where parking is already effectively controlled, such as in the New Forest.

7.26 The Government may wish to allow local authorities (subject to national guidance and regulation) to experiment further with such systems.

7.27 In taking forward its strategy for tourism,[5] the Government is well placed to develop a national framework to encourage the development of tourism in rural areas where the additional income is most needed. This could include a more strategic approach towards tourism, above and beyond current work on marketing and promotion. For example, the English Tourist Council and Regional Tourist Boards could target particular segments of the population to increase tourism in quieter periods outside school holidays. Some are already developing local sustainable tourist strategies.

7.28 The national effort should be supported at a regional level by efforts to exploit regional distinctiveness. Individual producers are often too small to carry the costs of developing a brand that might then add value to the product, and could usefully collaborate with other producers to promote area identities. In their economic strategies, RDAs should consider the key economic role

tourism can play within their regions. They also need to look for ways to attract more tourism (both in terms of spend per capita and, where appropriate, total numbers). The new regional Cultural Consortia (being set up by Department of Culture, Media and Sport) will be well placed to contribute to this.

7.29 For the reasons already mentioned, small operators are unlikely to be able to afford to market their business very effectively. There are significant opportunities, however, to market through the formation of co-operatives and to take advantage of new information technology to reach wider markets. Internet-based marketing is a cheap and effective way of reaching a potentially enormous number of customers.

7.30 Seaside towns could have a potentially important role to play within local rural development strategies, particularly in more geographically peripheral areas (such as Devon, Cornwall, Norfolk and Lincolnshire). But seaside resorts have been declining in terms of attracting tourist expenditure in recent years. Their traditional market was family-oriented, good-value holidays – a market sector that has been declining with the rise of cheap holidays abroad. Some resorts have succeeded by targeting niche markets and weekend breaks, or by creating 'all-year, all-weather' attractions. Many resorts have already been successful in attracting regeneration funding via the Government's Single Regeneration Budget or from other challenge funding initiatives. Such initiatives have placed tourism firmly in the forefront of social and economic regeneration priorities in those areas.

7.31 An example of how government can facilitate growth in rural tourism is highlighted in Box 7E.

[5] DCMS (1999), *Tomorrow's Tourism.*

Box 7E: Government Support for Tourism:

Devon Farms Liaison Group – Objective 5b Farm Tourism Project

The Devon Farms' Accommodation Group, consists of some 100 working farms that provide B&B and/or self catering tourist accommodation. Objective 5b funding has been available to improve marketing, business support and improved communication for the co-operative (although only 34 farms fall within the objective 5b area). The group raised nearly £25,000 themselves which was supported by £39,000 EAGGF funding and matched by £39,000 MAFF funding.

The individuals involved in the project (usually farmers' wives) have developed business skills as well as the skills necessary to operate in the tourism industry (e.g. marketing, administration, health and safety). In addition, they have built up a network which provides a supportive environment from which members' confidence can be built and new skills developed and recognised.

The particular challenges faced by members were associated with a lack of business skills within the Group when they started, to enable them to run their businesses effectively. For example, some providers were not taking their overhead costs into consideration when they calculated their prices. The group has organised training events to encourage members to price their accommodation in a more business-like way.

The Group is making increasing use of the Internet as a shared tool for marketing (the proportion of bookings made over the Internet is currently 5-10% and increasing rapidly). In addition, they have expanded their marketing efforts and published a booklet that has been sent to the main tourist information outlets in Birmingham, and the South of England.

Regulation

Reducing the regulatory burden on rural businesses

7.32 In recent years, concerns about the environmental and landscape impacts of farming, and concerns about the safety and wholesomeness of food, have led to more intervention by local, national and European Union policy-makers and enforcement authorities. For example, in terms of labour-market regulation, agriculture is the only sector of the UK economy to have regulation of its wages above and beyond that required under the National Minimum Wage, via the work of the Agricultural Wages Board. And where food safety is concerned, it is right that consumers should be entitled to high standards of quality, safety and reliability. But the increase in regulation in recent years introduced to achieve this has meant that

rural businesses have not benefited from the drive for a less burdensome regulatory regime for business. In short, the current levels, form and cost of regulation require further investigation.

7.33 The Government needs to remain vigilant in its attempts to maintain and raise standards without jeopardising the viability of the farming and food industries. If it fails to do so, not only will rural economies and communities suffer, but the very objectives of the intervention may be thwarted. The Government has to use all means that it has to both achieve high standards within the UK throughout the food chain, which command the support of consumers and the wider public, but also to work with other countries to raise standards worldwide.

7.34 Vigilance also requires the Government frequently to look for opportunities to reduce the regulatory burden in the agriculture and food processing sectors. This does not mean a lowering in protection for the environment or human health. Burdens can stem from requirements to deliver the objectives of the regulation: equally, they can arise from confusing and unnecessary provisions, reporting requirements, record keeping, or equipment which does not actually deliver better protection. The Government has taken an important step towards identifying and eliminating the latter with the announcement in September 1999 of a review of the regulatory burden on the agriculture sector. Further phases of this review could explore: the need for regulation; the effectiveness of regulations; the extent to which regulations are justified by market requirements; the economy and efficiency with which regulations are implemented and enforced; and the feasibility of alternatives to regulation. There may be merit in exploring the scope for the introduction of self-regulation systems and accreditation schemes (such as those run by the British Standards Institute).

7.35 More broadly, rural economies face a distinctive regulatory challenge on account of the predominance of small and micro-businesses. Businesses in rural areas are overwhelmingly small (over 90% employ fewer than 10 employees); and SMEs in rural areas tend to be smaller than those in urban areas – the 1997 Centre for Business Research survey showed rural SMEs to be smaller both in terms of median employment (8 against 13), and in terms of median turnover (£500,000 against £750,000). As regulation is largely a fixed cost, it impacts harder on smaller firms, and thus disproportionately in rural areas. The Cabinet Office's Regulatory Impact Unit (RIU) is currently exploring ways by which regulation can be made more sensitive to the circumstances of small and micro-businesses: these efforts should be maintained with a view to generating policy proposals at the earliest possible stage. Any policy proposals will need to be rural-

proofed, to ensure they address the specific challenges of small firms in rural areas; and there may be a case for including some rural areas within any initiatives set up to pilot regulatory reform.

Planning

7.36 The decline of agriculture and other primary industries as sources of employment and wealth creation poses difficulties for many rural settlements in more agriculturally-dependant areas. If rural communities are to survive, then they must be able to develop, attract and sustain new economic activities. The challenge lies in ensuring that these new activities do not destroy the distinctive character of the rural environment – not only because this is what many people value most about rural areas, but also because it is a source of competitive advantage for many rural businesses. This challenge is properly a matter for government: leaving everything to the market would lead to rapid degradation of the countryside.

7.37 The planning system is one of the key tools available to government in its attempts to meet the challenge. But too often planning is seen as a battle between commercial development and presevation of the countryside. In fact, this is a false division. Certainly, some kinds of development risk harming the environment and the landscape. But blocking all development – trying to "stop the clock" – risks leaving rural communities to wither. It can prevent local economies from generating the resources they need to maintain the local environment. For example, blocking development in villages may lead to greater commuting to nearby towns, or to the loss of key rural services such as schools and post offices.

7.38 Most decisions on planning are taken locally. The Government issues planning guidance – in particular, the text of Planning

Policy Guidance Note 7 (PPG7) on land-use planning in rural areas – and there are statutory instruments related to planning, notably the Use Classes Order. But it is for local planing authorities to interpret the guidance – in their development plans, and in their handling of, and decisions on, individual planning application.

7.39 Recent research,[6] recent surveys[7] and recent consultation exercises (for example, the one undertaken in early 1999 for the Rural White Paper) suggests that many local authorities apply non-statutory environmental designations (for example, 'green wedges' and 'strategic gaps') that can limitthe opportunities for economic growth in rural areas. The RDC report also highlights examples of planning applications for equestrian uses, farm diversification, recreation and tourism proposals and transport facilities for rural and urban residents all being refused on the grounds that they would constitute "inappropriate" development in the countryside.

7.40 The report also comments that 'Many authorities continue to operate a very strong presumption against uses not directly related to farming the land. Schemes are refused as unrelated to the needs of agriculture, forestry, the extraction of minerals or the disposal of waste.'[8] These findings are supported by the 1999 NFU survey, which observed that 'The most frequently stated problem was being refused permission to re-use agriculture buildings in order to diversify into other businesses to supplement the farm income'.[9] Such behaviour does not fit with the new economic realities of economic life in rural areas, where there has been considerable diversification out of primary production and into the manufacturing and service sectors.

7.41 Local and regional variation is one of the great strengths of the planning system. For example, the kind of development pressures – for more houses, more jobs, more leisure facilities – which many rural districts in the south-east experience would be welcome in many remote rural areas where unemployment, isolation and social decay are the great threats. But the over-restrictive approach which some planning authorities apply can inhibit development and agricultural diversification. It can also undermine the very vision of the countryside it seeks to protect, for instance by preventing sensitive infill housing of the kind which would bring families into a village, or allow the children of villagers to be able to afford to live in the community of their birth. Overly protected villages risk becoming dormitories for nearby towns or weekend retreats, rather than living and working communities.

7.42 Appropriate development based on sustainable development principles can be of positive benefit to the rural environment, even in National Parks and Areas of Outstanding Natural Beauty that are at times viewed as 'off-limits' to development. But the overall message from the RDC research is that, in practice, the planning system – as currently operated by some local authorities – is giving protection to open spaces regardless of the environment, economic or social outcomes of the proposal. In so doing, it is failing to match the principles of sustainable development, which seeks to reconcile all three to maximise the benefit for this and future generations.

7.43 Within the existing framework of land-use planning, the most effective means of achieving long-term change is through altering attitudes and beliefs. Officials, elected representatives and the communities they serve may benefit from better guidance on

---

[6] Rural Development Commission (1998) *Rural development and land-use planning policies.*

[7] NFU (1999) Survey of a sample of its members, the findings of which were published in the paper *Cutting Red Tape.*

[8] RDC, Op cit.

[9] NFU, Op cit.

how social, economic and environmental goals can be reconciled. In particular, those involved in land-use planning in rural areas need to be aware of the importance of farm diversification and the fact that that rural economic activity can not only be compatible with the cause of enhancing the rural environment but can also be helpful to it. More generally, change would be assisted by greater use of local deliberative processes that take a strategic, holistic and long-term approach to the issue of development in an area, perhaps starting with the question 'what development does our area need – and what share of regional and national development ought it to take – to ensure that it thrives in economic, environmental and social terms?'

7.44 Such processes, particularly if they were successful in involving all sections of the community rather than merely the vociferous minorities, could yield very different approaches to planning and answers to problems than is the case at present. Over time, effective processes of this nature could also reduce the need for detailed national regulation. Ideally, national guidance should give a clear statement of strategic direction (and an indication of the national and regional imperatives for development that need to be addressed) within which local deliberative processes can then shape local decision-making.

7.45 Striking this improved balance between deliberative processes and regulations will involve pursuing reforms at local and national level. Chapter 8 contains ideas for improving local processes. At the national level, Government could consider revising existing planning machinery – notably its planning guidance (in particular, the text of PPG7) and the Use Classes Order. Changes in national guidance could:

- provide stronger and more detailed guidance to planning authorities on the importance of fostering sympathetic and appropriate economic activity in rural areas – not least in maintaining rural environments;

- support local planning authorities in their work to allow appropriate development by producing an illustrative list (which would not be exhaustive) of economic activities that the Government believes to be appropriate in rural areas;

- require a stronger commitment to the desirability of change of commercial use, diversification and new commercial development on existing commercial sites (including farms).

7.46 There is also an option of assisting farm diversification while also introducing better protection for the rural landscape by bringing farms further into the orbit of the planning system, and in return allowing farmers more flexibility over change of use and the conversion of redundant farm buildings for commercial purposes. One option could be to place farms within the B1 Use Class, thereby allowing farmers to use their existing buildings to diversify into certain light-industrial activities, without the need for planning permission (though farmers will, of course, still need planning permission for new construction and engineering works associated with such permitted changes of use). Another could be to remove barriers to the conversion of redundant farm buildings for commercial purposes (in particular, by reviewing the continuing need for all the conditions listed in PPG7 para 3.14 and annex G). Such changes are significant and should therefore be considered only after careful evaluation of the risks and benefits.

7.47 To complement these ideas and suggestions, Chapter 8 of this report explores the development and introduction of new national arrangements to protect areas of the greatest environmental value.

7.48 Significant economic growth may bring with it pressures for residential development, and such pressures would need to be managed carefully. But the needs of rural areas are not served by large amounts of new development. Rather, they can best be met by new ways of diversifying and bolstering rural employment opportunities at the same time as maintaining safeguards on unnecessary or inappropriate development. Taken together, the ideas in this section could remove a number of the regulatory barriers to greater economic dynamism without jeopardising the quality of the rural environment. Together with other reforms to improve local deliberative processes, they could significantly improve the prospects for rural areas achieving sustainable development.

Improving regional planning guidance

7.49 The draft Planning Policy Guidance Note 11 (PPG11) on regional planning is currently being finalised by the DETR following consultation earlier this year. In finalising PPG11 it is essential to ensure that the guidance places sufficient weight on rural issues and encourages regional planning conferences, where appropriate, to develop sub-regional strategies for rural areas (for example, where there is a need for area-based regeneration programmes). More generally, it is vital that regional planning bodies act on the advice

concerning the need for regional planning guidance to take account of the RDAs' strategies and provide a spatial framework that allows for their implementation. And regional planning should ensure that local planning policies are sufficiently flexible on the prescriptions of development land to facilitate the sustainable growth of clusters of companies undertaking similar or associated activities in rural areas. Finally, in identifying areas of environmental importance, regional planning guidance should highlight the fact that appropriate forms of development may be needed to help sustain these areas.

Reducing planning restrictions on the use of agricultural land

7.50 As well as protection, the planning system places various forms of restriction on the agriculture sector: but one of the most prominent is the special status it affords to a significant proportion of agricultural land. Throughout the post-war period, the Government's planning guidance has included a presumption against the development of 'best and most versatile' (BMV) land – namely, land of high

Box 7F – Agricultural land classification: the existing system

Throughout the post-war period, it has been Government policy to protect the best and most versatile agricultural land as a resource for the future. Land uses which would cause permanent loss of this productive potential should be avoided as far as possible.[10]

The classification is designed to inform local planning authorities as part of the strategic planning process. It is based on the extent to which physical and chemical characteristics impose long term physical limitations on agricultural use. Factors affecting the grade of land are climate, site and soil characteristics (and the interactions between them).

The system grades land according to versatility (the range of crops that can be grown) and yield (the productiveness of land) from 1 to 5 (1 is excellent and 5 is very poor). Land grade 3 has been divided into 3a and 3b. Land of grades 1,2 and 3a is considered 'best and most versatile' and for planning purposes there is a strong presumption against development. Together such land accounts for about 38% of total agricultural land in the UK (although it is unevenly distributed, with a greater proportion of the best and most versatile land in England).

---

[10] DETR: PP97, *Planning Policy Guidance, Note 7, Annex B: Development Involving Agriculture Land.*

agricultural quality. Since 1985, the BMV designation has covered all land in grades 1, 2 and 3a, approximately one-third of all agricultural land in England (see Box 7F). PPG7 requires planning authorities to 'include policies for the protection of the best and most versatile agricultural land'. This protection is reinforced by MAFF's powers, unique among Government Departments, to require intervention by DETR if MAFF believes that a draft local authority's draft plan will involve the loss of such land to other uses.

7.51 Within the post-war policy framework, where the Government sought to ensure security and sufficiency of food supply from domestic sources, the case for locking agricultural land into permanent agricultural use was strong. Once these assumptions are abandoned, the rationale for the policy is weaker, and the detrimental consequences of the policy become clearer. The most important of these is the barrier created to economic adjustment and the optimum allocation of resources. Farmers of BMV land who wish their land to be used for other economic activities are prevented from doing so, even if this change of use would result in a better outcome economically, socially and environmentally. This may delay some inefficient farmers' departure from the industry and prevent other farmers from diversifying to meet consumer needs in markets other than those for agricultural produce. Removing the protection for agricultural land would facilitate economic adjustment and diversity throughout all parts of rural England, rather than solely in those areas with lower grade agricultural land.

7.52 Those wishing to retain the protection for BMV land have argued that the one third of English agricultural land currently classified as BMV is a resource that should be guarded for future generations, who might need it if

the UK's requirements of land for basic food production were to change dramatically. But those arguing for change say that giving such land a higher protection than any other kind in fact works against finding the most sustainable outcome. They say that BMV land does not necessarily have a high environmental, biological or aesthetic value: it often consists of large, open fields given over to producing the greatest possible quantity of commodity crops. They believe that, as a result, BMV protection has resulted in development taking place on more environmentally valuable land such as water meadows and heathland.

7.53 Making the removal of protection for BMV land dependent on the introduction of a new national framework for protecting areas of high environmental value could be one way of providing reassurance and constitute a significant improvement on the current BMV arrangements. Using the framework of objectives proposed in Chapter 6, a powerful case can be made for a national framework of environmental criteria that could protect the land of high environmental value – an approach explored in Chapter 8. As mentioned above, environmental and agricultural value are not synonymous. So, removing the protection for BMV land could, over time, lead to a wider range of development in areas of reasonable agricultural productivity but low landscape or amenity value. But a new system of environmental protection might lead to a narrower range of development in areas that are less productive for agriculture but have significant habitat or biodiversity and landscape value. In effect, such an approach would shift the focus of Government away from the old priority of maximising agricultural production and towards its new priorities in relation to the environment. Given the potential gain for the countryside and rural communities, the Government might consider further evaluation of this issue.

7.54 Even small scale changes to land use classification are certain to raise concerns about the impact on those rural areas where development pressures are most intense. But removing the protection for BMV land need not lead to additional physical development. The amount of housing in rural areas will be determined principally by the government's targets for the location of future household growth. The Government recognises the seriousness of the the threat to rural England of over-development. That is why it has set a target for at least 60% of all new homes to be built on brownfield sites. Moreover, in its forthcoming Urban White Paper the Government will be responding to the many suggestions of the Urban Task Force on how to ensure that cities become places where people want to live, work and stay. These measures will allow the Government to restrict the amount of new housing development that has to take place on greenfield sites. But the issue raised by BMV protection is not to do with the *amount* of new development: rather, it is about *where any agreed amount of new development goes.* At present, BMV agricultural land is protected from development – whereas land of high environmental value may not be. Changing these regulations would allow local authorities to ensure that suitable applications for development could be steered to sites so that the stock of local environmental value was maximised.

7.55 Perhaps most importantly, the key local protections against inappropriate development would remain in place. Planning applications would still be determined in accordance with the Local Plan, which has to conform with the Structure Plan and take account of national guidance (including Regional Planning Guidance, which has indicated the number of new housing units that different parts of the country may bear). So the removal of protection for BMV land would not, for

example, change the number of new houses being built. What it could do is create more flexibility in where those houses might go. New housing, as with other forms of development, could be accommodated more easily and with a greater overall benefit for rural communities. In any case, the changes would not be quick; and, where change occurred, the decisions would be taken by local planning authorities – not by individual farmers and developers.

Bringing all agricultural development within planning control

7.56 Another aspect of the special treatment afforded to agriculture within the post-war period was its partial exclusion from the planning system. As noted in Chapter 4, the 1947 Town and Country Planning Act excluded the use of land for agriculture from the definition of development; and agricultural buildings and other development benefited from generous permitted development rights or PDRs. Since 1992, the Government has undertaken a programme of piecemeal reforms that has partially removed this special treatment. But the resulting series of regulations is complex, confusing and burdensome to both farmers and planning officials. Under the present arrangements:

- agricultural buildings over a certain height and/or within a certain distance of a road, residential property or school require planning permission;

- in National Parks, Areas of Outstanding Natural Beauty and Conservation Areas, PDRs have been reduced or withdrawn;

- throughout the country, local authorities can ask the permission of the Secretary of State for Environment, Transport and the Regions to withdraw PDRs if they believe there is a real and specific threat to the rural landscape;

- some PDRs have been withdrawn for agricultural holdings of less than 5 hectares – so, for example, a planning application is required for a new building, but not for an extension or alteration;

- local authorities can direct the removal of buildings constructed under PDRs if they cease to be used for agricultural purposes within 10 years and planning permission is not granted for re-use.

7.57 The net result – combining both exemption on the one hand and additional rules on the other – is complex and illogical. The case for continuing exemption via the planning system for agricultural buildings is weak. Replacing the regime of partial PDRs with one where all agricultural buildings required planning permission would ensure equality and clarity. It would also allow planning authorities to prevent environmentally inappropriate development in agriculture in exactly the same way as they can with such development in other sectors of the economy. Given the complexity of the PDR regime, this reform is consistent with the Government's commitment to better regulation.

7.58 The principal argument against change is that full inclusion within the planning system might place undue restriction on farmers' freedom to expand, diversify and change use. But if these freedoms are desirable, then they are desirable for all economic activities that take place in rural areas – and the aspects of the planning system that block these freedoms should be reformed. Such a programme of reform was explored above. Nevertheless, the Government might wish to ensure that the planning framework (in particular, the national planning guidance) is properly aligned with the policy of allowing farmers greater commercial freedom before bringing all aspects of agricultural development into the system.

8. SUSTAINING AND ENHANCING THE RURAL ENVIRONMENT

Summary

The British public has a strong attachment to the countryside, but the nature of that attachment continues to change. The traditional landscape of fields, woods and villages is still valued, but other concerns – such as the strength of rural communities, biodiversity, or access to the countryside – have grown in importance over the last fifty years.

If the Government policy is to ensure England's rural environment remains a source of beauty, wealth and pride – with greater protection for what is valued most – then policies have to change as well. There is a need to introduce a more sophisticated approach to environmental policy-making which takes full account of the complex interrelationships between the economy, rural communities and the environment, and is based on the principles of sustainability.

The chapter outlines the range of policy instruments that could be of assistance in achieving rural environmental objectives and managing the complex balances and trade-offs that need to be struck, including ways to encourage local community involvement in decision-making and a new national framework for protecting land of environmental value.

Introduction

8.1   Opinion polling repeatedly demonstrates that the British public feels a strong attachment to the rural environment. Some 91% of respondents polled for the Countryside Commission in 1997 agreed that "society has a moral duty to protect the countryside for future generations"[1].

In February 1999 Gallup found that 71% of people believed the quality of life is better in the countryside than in towns and cities and 66% of people said they would move there if there were no obstacles to doing so[2]. There is also a widespread concern that the quality of the rural environment is deteriorating.

[1]   Countryside Commission (1997) *Public Attitudes to the Countryside*, CCP481, Cheltenham: Countryside Agency, p.6.
[2]   Gallup (1999) *Rural Economy Survey: An Analysis of People's Views and Attitudes to the Countryside*, London: Strutt & Parker.

8.2   The quality of the rural environment is clearly an issue of concern to many people. However, what counts as 'the environment' must be carefully defined to avoid confusion. Rural environmental public goods can be divided into five main components, as follows:–

- **Biodiversity** – (plant and animal species and their habitats).

- **Natural resources** – (in particular, air, soil and water quality).

- **Landscapes** – very few of which are wholly 'natural' in England, but are more commonly the product of land and landscape management practices.

- **Cultural heritage** – such as valued ancient monuments.

- **Public access and enjoyment** – the ability to access and enjoy the countryside.

8.3   What is valued about 'the rural environment' is not fixed over time. Popular representations about 'the countryside' change, especially over the longer term, along with prevailing social values. For example, while the dominant representation of the Lake District in the seventeenth century was as a barren, isolated and desolate place, it is now seen as a 'national treasure' with a landscape of great beauty. Prevailing ideas and values about environmental attributes not only change over time, but also vary between different social groups. What might be termed a weed or pest by one group could be seen as a valuable component of local bio-diversity by another.

Change in the countryside

8.4   The implication of this analysis is that what counts as 'environmentally valuable' varies over time and between different groups in society, just as the countryside itself has always been subject to change. As a result, particular pieces of environmental

policy will reflect the dominant concerns of their day or of particular social interests.

8.5   The post-war policy framework for the protection of the rural environment is no exception to this rule. The framework is a product of its age and is predicated upon a very particular view of what was valuable and to be protected. The dominant concerns of the day were to expand food production and to provide a secure business environment for farmers to achieve this. A prosperous and productive agriculture was seen as an important element of the stewardship of the countryside, and the main threat to the rural environment was seen as urban sprawl. The consequence of this particular view of the rural environment was that those areas of strongest development control in rural areas were Green Belts around the major cities, and the National Parks (which were confined to the agriculturally marginal uplands).

8.6   There is a growing recognition that society should value and protect environmental attributes in all the categories listed above, and widespread acceptance that environmental policy should prioritise access as well as conservation. This consensus is much more wide-ranging and sophisticated than the prevailing opinion in the 1940s. But the Government's policy framework is based on the view from the 1940s. It needs to be modernised, so that Government is properly equipped to sustain and enhance the rural environment.

8.7   The view that nothing must be allowed to change would spell disaster for the rural environment. Change is inevitable, in the economy (such as new patterns of employment), society (such as increased leisure time) and the environment itself (where climate change is likely to bring significant changes to biodiversity and to the landscape over the coming decades). Simply preserving the rural landscape exactly as it is today is not an option and trying to do so would only lead to mismanagement of these inevitable changes.

8.8   Moreover, some changes to the landscape can help to improve environmental quality. For example, some lowland agricultural landscapes, some former coalfield areas, and some areas of industrial forestry would benefit from environmental regeneration to improve the quality of the landscape. Even industrial uses, properly managed, can bring benefits, as where old quarries are developed to form nature reserves. The Norfolk Broads – one of the most precious sites in England for wildlife and for tourism – are entirely man-made excavations which have since flooded and produced eco-systems of great value.

Sustaining and enhancing the rural environment

8.9   The Government's strategy for rural economies should be based on the principles of sustainability, subsidiarity and flexibility. The Government should aim to foster economic development that sits comfortably with (and seeks, where possible, to enhance) the rural environment and the quality of life for rural communities. In accordance with the Government's commitment to sustainable development, the strategy should ensure that the current generation does not use the resources available to it in a way which prejudices the opportunities of future generations. And the strategy should seek to find ways of reconciling the competing demands of economic, environmental and social objectives. In practice, this approach would encourage and support what the CPRE has termed 'discerning development'[3].

8.10   The real strategic challenge lies not just in developing the principles of sustainable development – or gaining political support

for them. It lies in interpreting these principles, to determine where the balance between competing (and sometimes conflicting) objectives should be. In practice, the rural environment must; provide high air, soil and water quality; maintain biodiversity and valued landscapes; provide for the sustainable production of food and other products; provide for the sustainable management of other natural resources; and support the protection of historic and cultural features. These objectives must be reconciled with the needs of local communities as well as the needs of the wider economy and society.

8.11   This overarching strategy for the rural environment can be translated into practicable and effective policy only if the Government is adequately informed about development and trends within the rural environment and if options and choices are brought into focus by the specifics of environmental indicators and targets. There is currently a great deal of work within Government to provide the information necessary to inform rural environmental policy-making. The DETR is working to develop indicators of sustainable development at a national level to inform national policy decisions. MAFF is developing a set of sustainable agriculture indicators in parallel, and the Countryside Agency has developed 'Countryside Character' maps which map out local diversity and distinctiveness. There remains a need, however, to develop indicators which can be used at regional and local level to inform policy choices in rural areas and which are meaningful and of value to local communities.

8.12   To deliver sustainable development the Government will need a broad range of environmental tools and instruments that help safeguard the environment against the wide variety of economic and social pressures that face rural areas. In applying such tools

3   CPRE (1998), *Country Values: Valued Country.*

Government needs to consider the potential distortions and inefficiencies that can occur. (Annex A3 explores the rationale and principles determining Government action and considers both the circumstances the range of instruments available to the Government looks at these issues in more detail.)

8.13 In addition, Government needs to acknowledge that in many cases it will not be appropriate for it to act as the sole or prime agent in the delivery of environmental policy, and that local communities have a strong role to play in shaping their own strategies. And, where the Government can play a principal or leading role it will need to ensure that it is properly equipped with the necessary tools and instruments – in terms of regulation, taxes and charges, and expenditure programmes – to implement the strategy. So the agenda for the Government is fourfold:

i) encouraging and enabling local solutions to environmental challenges;

ii) updating the regulatory framework;

iii) assessing the range of taxation and charging options available to help further environmental objectives; and

iv) ensuring that expenditure programmes are appropriately tailored towards the strategy for the rural environment.

Encouraging and enabling local solutions

8.14 Encouraging local involvement in both decision-making and delivery is an important part of the strategy for enhancing and sustaining the rural environment. It is important that environmental problems are addressed at the right level – national, regional or local, using the most appropriate mix of instruments to tackle them. Key implications of this are:

- at a national level, government needs to establish the overall policy framework (e.g. through national environmental designations, the PPG mechanism or by providing environmental incentives);

- at regional level there is a need to develop strategies to tailor policies to meet regional development objectives (e.g. through the RDAs' Regional Economic Strategies and the new Rural Development plans); and

- at local level, community involvement and ownership and participation is vital (e.g. through local appraisal schemes which can be used to identify local economic, social and environmental objectives).

8.15 This section of the Chapter will concentrate on the scope for improving local processes, in particular, identifying those tools and approaches that can help to include those sections of the community which might otherwise be marginalised by decision-making processes.

8.16 Local appraisal schemes are a useful tool for effective local decision-making on environmental issues. They allow local communities to come to a collective view about what type of environment they would like and what the balance of environmental, economic and social conditions for a given area should be. Care needs to be taken by regional and local government bodies to ensure local people's views are incorporated into decision-making, and to ensure that 'top-down' and 'bottom-up' approaches can be successfully meshed.

8.17 Over the past 20 years more than 1500 rural communities in Britain have 'taken stock' using local appraisal methods. A recent report concluded that local appraisals are 'arguably now the most significant single tool of community development in contemporary Britain'.[4] Box 8A presents a local community

---

[4] Moseley (1997), *Parish Appraisals as a tool of Rural Community Development.*

Box 8A: Letcombe Bassett Village Appraisal

Letcombe Bassett is a small but lively village with a population of 160. A long history has not spared Letcombe Bassett from rural depopulation and declining services. In 1949 Berkshire County Council decided to relocate the residents. To quote from the report *"Bassett would, in effect, revert to a little group of farms with associated dwellings…"*. The village rose up in wrath under the slogan *"Letcombe Bassett is too old to die"*. The decision was overturned.

The village school and pub have since closed, but when the shop was threatened with closure, it was replaced by a community shop run by volunteers.

"The idea of holding a Village Appraisal was prompted by a visit from Oxfordshire Rural Community Council in 1997. Responses were received from around 70% of residents, with 12 completely blank forms returned, indicating that not everyone supported the appraisal. Entering data into a computer was done in pairs by appraisal committee members (and their teenage children). Entering and analysing the results took far longer than expected. We also forgot to apply for funding, so had to pay for the questionnaire printing ourselves! The major findings were reported to a Village Meeting in June 1998, with a lively debate about the lack of a village pub and what to do about it."

Positive Outcomes

- A regular village newsletter and an information sheet has been established.
- A major review of the Community Shop has taken place, with improved stock and more flexible opening – its survival is, however, still in the balance.
- The Neighbourhood Watch scheme has been extended.
- Renewed interest in village history and community has resulted.
- Improvements to the Village Hall– subject to a *Millennium Festival Award.*

Negative Outcomes

- Some suggestions aroused hostility, especially relating to private property – e.g. why should the pub re-open when the owners don't want it to?
- Failure to achieve results on traffic and planning creates a feeling of impotency.
- Despite the enthusiasm from some, others remain apathetic.

"The overall view was that the appraisal was a worthwhile project, which has involved many residents in taking more interest in the village's past and future."

perspective on the process, (with some of the text written by the individuals from Letcombe Bassett village who organised the appraisal).

8.18 Recent experience in Oxfordshire (Box 8B) highlights some of the long-term environmental benefits for the community of parish appraisal schemes. But the benefits are not simply environmental: they extend to the social and economic realms. For example, the improvement of the local environment

Box 8B: Evaluation of Oxfordshire Parish Appraisals

Oxfordshire Rural Community Council has supported parish appraisals for a number of years, and helped local groups to locate funding. They surveyed groups that had carried out the appraisal several years ago to identify what progress had been made.

The evidence was very positive. Different parishes identified a variety of priorities and objectives that suited their particular needs. The review highlighted the fact that the *process* of carrying out a parish appraisal is beneficial in itself in terms of community development, but also that the momentum generated by the process within the community can continue beyond the appraisal process.

As well as leading to the introduction of a number of new services, many villages identified improvements to the local environment as key priorities. Some examples of action taken following rural appraisals are;

- the village of Launton (population 2112) carried out an appraisal in 1993/4 and established an environmental group which surveyed and assessed local footpaths and developed an energy conservation project which won £6,000 to spend on community buildings; and

- Woodcote village (population 2500) identified litter management and dog fouling as priorities and as a result the Parish Council has organised more waste bins in the village and a fenced off children's play area. The village has seen the appraisal process as so valuable that they have repeated it several times.

generates feels of social well-being and community ownership[5].

8.19 Village Design Statements are another community-based approach developed to overcome the polarisation which can sometimes emerge between those who want to develop rural areas, and those who are concerned that the fabric and local distinctiveness of the countryside will be damaged by development. The exercises have two main functions. The first, and most significant function, is as a planning tool to enable communities to influence the formal planning process so that it can take account of local goals. The second, as with village appraisals, is to involve local people in decisions about the scale and direction of development in their area. The statements aim to move discussions away from a

polarised view of development (which posits the choice of either environmental protection or economic development), towards a view which accepts the need for rural communities to develop their own economy as well as support the local environment and community.

8.20 The concept stems from a critique of conventional analytical methodologies which called for an approach that 'instead of describing a particular design outcome, should outline a procedure that must be followed before the appropriate design outcome can be achieved'[6]. Again, as with local appraisals, the process is seen as key to securing the desired outcome.

8.21 Village Design Statements were conceived by the Countryside Commission

[5] Oxfordshire Rural Community Council (1999), *Monitoring the Medium to Longer Term Impacts of Parish Appraisals.*

[6] RDC (1994), *Planning for Better Rural Design.*

Box 8C: Management of the Local Environment by the Community: The Mourne Heritage Trust

The Trust is an unusual example of community led 'bottom-up' involvement in the management of a protected area. The Trust was launched in 1997 as a charitable company and is managed by a voluntary Board of Trustees, with the agreement of the core funding bodies who agreed a three-year funding allocation. The funding partners include Department for Agriculture Northern Ireland (DANI), Northern Ireland Environment and Heritage Department, the Local District Councils and the Northern Ireland Tourist Board.

In addition to employing rangers and activities such as organising repair of footpaths, the trust delivers on behalf of DANI a £425,000 programme of grant aid to rural regeneration initiatives through the Mourne Area Based Strategy. The Trust also provides an environmental management strategy within the area designated as an AONB in 1986.

The organisation's history extends back to a community-led environmental campaign to oppose the construction of a dam in the area. Opposition to the dam was successful and the area was proposed for AONB status which required an environmental management programme. The Northern Ireland Environment and Heritage Department supported the creation of the Trust as the body to take this programme forward and, although statutory responsibility for delivery of the strategy remains with the Environment Department, it is delivered by the Trust.

in 1993, and although they are still relatively new, research suggests that they are gaining support. A recent report[7] suggests that the role of village design statements as part of the planning process can be very positive and that, where statements are developed, they are widely used by local planning authorities, architects, builders and developers. In addition, they enable communities to articulate what makes their locality distinctive, and therefore what features are particularly valued.

8.22 The potential for community-based action is not confined to needs assessment and planning: there is also scope for community-led implementation and management of environmental schemes and programmes. Such schemes are a valuable means of nurturing and strengthening the stock of environmental public goods, especially in the section of the

rural landscape that is not being farmed (and therefore not amenable to the agriculture-specific policies for the provision of public goods as described in chapter 9). A practical example of communities working together to develop their own ideas about how they would like their local environment managed is the Mourne Heritage Trust in Northern Ireland (see Box 8C, above). In England, the Countryside Agency will be reintroducing the Rural Action for the Environment scheme (previously run by the Countryside Commission) with effect from 2000. The new scheme will reflect the imperative of targeting resources at needs that are currently not met through other sources of funding, such as the National Lottery. It will distribute resources through rural action grants, probably working through Rural Community Councils.

---

[7] Owen (1998), *The role of Village Design Statements in fostering a locally responsive approach to village planning and design in the UK*, Journal of Urban Design, Vol. 3 No. 3, 359–380.

8.23 At a local level, Local Authorities are perhaps the most significant agent in delivering sustainable development. Local Agenda 21 'has emerged as the principal means of addressing sustainable development in practice'.[8] It provides the means by which local authorities can incorporate the principles of sustainable development into their work. It can also be used by local communities as a way of identifying their long-term economic, environmental and social requirements from their local authority. The Government's recent White Paper on Sustainable Development[9] set out the clear role the Government identifies for Local Agenda 21 in delivering its sustainable development principles. In 1997, the Prime Minister set a target for all local authorities to have Local Agenda 21 strategies in place by the year 2000. In addition, government is proposing to give local authorities a new power to promote the economic, social and environmental well being of their areas.

8.24 Most Local Agenda 21 processes are led by local authorities with the involvement of local community groups, but there is no single model for developing strategies. Some local authorities have gone further and encouraged local community groups to come together to draw up the plans themselves. Gloucestershire County Council, for example, has substantially delegated the work of developing the Local Agenda 21 strategy to a local charity. Reading Borough Council has developed its strategy in close liaison with the Worldwide Fund for Nature and the Community Education Development Centre which has resulted in a neighbourhood-based approach.

8.25 Where Local Agenda 21 strategies are developed in a genuinely participatory way, and adequate political and financial weight is given to the project, then there is potential for the strategies to play a very valuable role.

There is a risk, however, that not all local authorities accord the process as much value as they should and the 'environment' becomes marginalised as a result so the opportunity to build in environmental considerations into mainstream policy making is lost.

Updating the regulatory framework

8.26 There are a number of regulatory changes which could further environmental objectives for rural areas.

a) Developing a new framework and methodology for protecting land of high environmental value

8.27 Rural districts account for 88% of the total land-mass of land in England. Some 75% of the land area in England is used for agriculture. Chapter 4 explained that the desire to provide a secure food supply in the post-war period laid the policy framework for agriculture, and Chapter 7 went on to describe the system to protect higher quality agricultural lands (see Box 7F for further details).

8.28 As the earlier section pointed out, the existing classification system has been successful in keeping land in agricultural use, but has restricted farmers' ability to develop or dispose of land for non-agricultural purposes.

8.29 In addition, it has tended to encourage economic development on land which is less productive agriculturally. The land classification system is not designed to take the environmental value of the land into account, despite the fact that land which is less productive agriculturally may be of significant environmental value in terms of species diversity or landscape features.

[8] Selman & Parker (1999), *Tales of Local Sustainability.*

[9] DETR (1999), *A better Quality of Life.*

8.30 The existing regime makes sense only in the context of the post-war paradigm for rural policy: when assessed with reference to the concerns and priorities in the late 1990s, the case for change is strong. But change should not remove the capacity for identifying and protecting valuable land – rather, it should update the definition of what is valued, to reflect today's environmental concerns (which are not about agricultural productivity and the supply of food).

8.31 The Government needs a new approach to identifying and protecting land of value in the countryside. Box 8D outlines some of the factors and issues which would need to be considered. The purpose of a new framework is not to employ large numbers of staff in an exhaustive survey of every acre of land with a view to producing a map that classifies the whole of England into a list of environmental categories: rather, it is to ensure that areas of high environmental value are identified and recognised in the decisions of central and local government. Developing a new national framework will require: the continuation of key components of existing protection – for example, National Parks; the bringing together of expertise from a wide range of sources within government organisations; consultation with local authorities and interest groups; and careful piloting to evaluate the feasibility of proposals. But the potential rewards from a new framework – in terms of protecting what

Box 8D: A new way of valuing land in the countryside

A new framework would need to:

- be based on the principles of sustainable development and include an assessment of the economic (including agriculture as well as other economic activities), environmental and community value of the land (including amenity, recreation and access as well as cultural and historic features);

- recognise that land is a finite resource and hence there will be competing activities for its use in some areas – so criteria will be needed to adjudicate between competing claims;

- recognise that the rural landscape is largely a product of agricultural and other land management practices and, as they change, so will the landscape;

- be flexible enough to take into account the possible consequences of future changes to local circumstances and priorities;

- take account of local distinctiveness of the land (perhaps drawing on the Countryside Agency's 'Countryside Character' maps and descriptions and Village Design Schemes); and

- give stronger protection to land of exceptional environmental value (on the basis of biodiversity of historic landscapes, for example).

In addition, work is needed to design a mechanism to draw all the elements together so that it can inform planning processes and decisions in a meaningful way at both national and local levels.

A new framework could enhance the protection for land of great environmental value which falls outside existing protection (i.e. AONBs, National Parks, SSSIs and ESAs). However, it could also free up land of less environmental value which has hitherto been protected solely on the basis of its agricultural function.

is valued most in the rural environment – are substantial. Should the new framework prove practicable, there would be a case for reviewing the need for the existing proliferation of local designations, many of which have been introduced by local authorities because of their views that the protection offered at national level is insufficiently fine-grained.

b) Cost and Benefits of Planning Approval

8.32 Simply granting planning permission can have an enormous impact on the value of land and buildings. This windfall gain is reaped once development takes place – in part by the landowner, but also by the developer. The local community does not necessarily experience any of the benefit, but may experience environmental and other costs (e.g. increased traffic and demands on local services).

8.33 Currently planning gain mechanisms (under Section 106) are used to provide a means of mitigating the off-site effects of development (on-site impacts are considered within the planning application itself). Thus, the developer may agree to provide services or amenities (for example, an element of social housing, or a children's play area) to the local community as part of the approval of their planned development. However, the planning gain process can be opaque and open to the perception of abuse. It can also be the source of uncertainty, delay and inconsistency (across different local authorities) in the planning process. Moreover, it often fails to *directly* address the off-site effects it is intended to capture.

8.34 Thus there is scope for a more effective mechanism to capture these off-site effects, that could at the same time improve the planning process. Two such mechanisms are offsetting and impact fees.

8.35 Offsetting involves developers being required to offset the external or off-site effects of the development. Offsetting is most commonly encountered in the context of the environmental impact of development. Thus, for example, if conversion of a barn from agricultural to housing status displaces barn owls, the developer would have a responsibility to provide an alternative nesting site; and the loss of an area of greenfield habitat might require the establishment of a (smaller) nature reserve in its place. The Countryside Agency has suggested a similar approach in the form of 'development obligations', in its recent report on planning in rural areas.[11]

8.36 Impact fees involve an explicit schedule of charges for the various external and off-site effects of development. Instead of providing redress in kind – as in planning gain and offsetting – the developer makes a cash payment to the local authority. This can directly capture the costs to the local authority (or indeed the economy or society more widely) of some of these off-site effects, such as increased demands on public services; and could provide the funding for local authorities to offset other effects, such as replacing lost habitats. It also provides the local authority with more flexibility over how these off-site effects are addressed, making it easier to reflect local needs, priorities and preferences.

8.37 Both impact fees and offsetting mechanisms have the potential to be more effective ways of capturing the off-site effects of development, and would be more transparent and certain in their application – reducing delay in the planning process. It would be useful for DETR to examine impact fees and offsetting in more detail, including the practicalities of implementing and applying them at the local level.

[11] Countryside Agency (September 1999), *Planning for Quality in Rural England*, pp13–14.

8.38 However, while planning gain, offsetting and impact fees help to capture the wider costs of planning approval, they fail to address the often substantial windfall gains that are also generated. These windfall gains are an appropriate target for government, as the windfall gains are the consequence of a government decision – to approve that planning application – and this approval is often the only feature distinguishing the particular site from others in the area. A tax on windfall gains is also efficient (in an optimal tax sense), as it does not distort behaviour. In this case, even quite high rates would still leave the value of land with planning approval much higher than that without.

8.39 Despite this strong rationale, taxes on the betterment of land (through development) have not always been successful in practice: witness, for example, the fate of development land taxes in 1970s. A potentially more credible way of imposing a tax on betterment would be the harmonisation of VAT rates on the construction of new dwellings (which is currently zero-rated) and on renovation and repair work to existing dwellings (which faces the full rate of VAT). This has been recommended by the Urban Task Force, not least to remove an apparent anomaly that may skew development towards new dwellings.[12] EU rules mean that once a zero-rated item is brought within VAT, the zero-rate cannot be reinstated (see, for example, VAT on domestic fuel), so the introduction of VAT on the construction of new dwellings would be credible. The Government shares the Urban Task Force's desire for an urban renaissance. It is carefully considering the recommendations in the report and will respond (primarily) in the forthcoming Urban White Paper.

c. Environmental charges and rebates

8.40 The 1999 Budget announced a presumption in favour of environmental taxes. The Treasury's statement of intent on environmental taxation states:

"The Government's central economic objectives are the promotion of high and sustainable levels of growth an high levels of employment. By that we mean that growth must be both stable and environmentally sustainable. Quality of growth matters; not just quantity.

"… Government will explore the scope for using the tax system to deliver environmental objectives – as one instrument, in combination with others. Over time, the government will aim to reform the tax system to increase incentives to reduce environmental damage. That will shift the burden of tax from 'goods' to 'bads'; encourage innovation in meeting higher environmental standards; and deliver a more dynamic economy and a cleaner environment, to the benefit of everyone.

"Where environmental measures meet the general tests of good taxation, the government will use them."

The economic rationale for such an approach is explored further in Annex A3.

8.41 In practice there are a number of potential environmental taxes and charges that could be evaluated to see if they could play a positive role in future policy. These have been (or are being) explored in other government policy documents and there is little for this report to add. There are also issues around the level of subsidies and rebates paid to particular sectors or attached to particular

---

[12] One concern about the proposal is that it will make new-build social housing more expensive for those on low incomes. But VAT on new-build need not drive up the rents of tenants in the social housing sector: the Social Housing Grant (SHG) to Registered Social Landlords is set at a level to sustain affordable rents – so any increase in the cost of building and running social housing should feed through to an increase in SHG, thereby avoiding any large rise in rents. In effect, some of any increase in the Government's income from higher VAT would be balanced by an increase in expenditure on grants for social housing.

products. An example of this is the rebate for gas oil and fuel oil for non road use (which includes heating), known as 'red diesel'. Red diesel accounts for about 25% of heavy oil use and bears a duty of 3.03 pence per litre compared with 47.21 pence for diesel for road use. The issue provides an incentive to use the rebate to evade the higher rate of duty. The issue has implications beyond rural policy – less than 10% of red diesel is used by agriculture and forestry – but there is a case for keeping these arrangements under review.

Public expenditure

8.42 The final instrument available to the Government for pursuit of its environmental objectives is expenditure: the Government can use tailored programmes to encourage and support activities that benefit the environment of rural areas. The Government's use of this instrument is extensive and wide-ranging – and extends well beyond farmers, reflecting the fact that the production of environmental

public goods is not the exclusive preserve of the agriculture industry. To take four examples: agri-environment programmes pay out over £100m to encourage more environmentally friendly farming; the environmental and rural agencies (in particular, English Nature and the Countryside Agency) fund a variety of programmes that enhance the environment of rural areas; national and local government bodies provide a range of grants to voluntary organisations engaged in environmental management; and the national regeneration programmes (in particular, those covered by the Single Regeneration Budget) have funded many environmental improvement schemes.

8.43 But there may be scope to make further use of expenditure programmes to help realise the Government's environmental objectives for rural areas. In particular, the Government will need to consider the case for using new EU resources over the medium-term – for the Rural Development Regulation and from the Structural Funds – on environmental schemes when drawing up its spending programmes.

9: DEVELOPING A COMPETITIVE, FORWARD-LOOKING, MODERNISED AGRICULTURAL INDUSTRY

Summary

Agricultural policy needs to encourage a competitive, forward-looking and modernised industry and to help the sector provide the goods and services that society wants – a well managed rural environment as well as efficiently produced and safe food.

Much of farming policy is set Europe-wide through the EU's Common Agricultural Policy, so this is the main forum for change. The recent Agenda 2000 reforms offer increased national discretion over how CAP resources can be deployed, allowing a switch of emphasis from production payments to support to farming which also meets environmental and rural development objectives.

Domestic policy in areas such as planning and regulation can also encourage farmers to add value to their operations. Through a combination of payments, deregulation and exhortation the Government could also increase assist the growth of the organic sector, the spread of farmers' markets and the development of locally differentiated and branded produce.

Introduction

9.1   Agriculture is the most important land user in rural areas. While its relative shares of GDP and employment have been in long-term decline, its total output has been increasing in absolute terms. The primary economic role of agriculture is, and will continue to be, the production of food. With continuing development as a market-orientated, productive and competitive industry, agriculture cannot merely survive, but can also thrive, as a supplier of food to domestic and international markets. But agriculture is a special sector of the economy precisely because it is not simply a producer of food: society values a range of environmental and aesthetic factors (for example, landscape and habitat) which farming influences, protects or has even created, even though farmers are not directly remunerated for many of these goods. The task for Government is to ensure that the agricultural industry is competitive, forward-looking and modernised to deliver the full set of goods and services that society now values.

There have already been significant steps in this direction and this chapter sets out an agenda for further reform. Central to this is the discretion now available to national governments as part of the 1999 reform of the CAP.

The CAP and national discretion

9.2   The recent Agenda 2000 reforms significantly increase the national discretion in the operation of the CAP (as shown in Box 9A). In several crucial respects, the direction in which the new CAP is implemented is now the choice of the UK and not the EU.

9.3   The Agenda 2000 reforms, agreed in March 1999, effectively extend the approach to CAP reform established in an earlier round of reforms in 1992. The approach is to reduce price support for agricultural commodities, but then compensate farmers for these price cuts through a system of direct compensation payments. The 1999 reforms deepened the price cuts introduced in 1992 and increased the associated compensation payments. In 1997/8, direct payments to farmers accounted for approximately £1.7 billion in England, or almost half of all CAP support, and this proportion is set to increase as a result of the Agenda 2000 reforms.[1]

9.4   The 1992 CAP reforms also introduced a set of 'accompanying measures' to the CAP to assist in the restructuring of the agricultural sector. These measures provided for support for agri-environmental schemes, farm afforestation and early retirement schemes. The 1999 reforms have expanded

Box 9A: After Berlin: CAP and national discretion

- Member States can decide how to implement the Rural Development Regulation (RDR), which will represent approximately 10% of CAP monies across the EU (though the UK has been allocated only a 3.5% share of the RDR budget). Of the nine sets of measures in the Regulation, Member States are obliged to implement the agri-environment measures, and can choose whether or not to implement the other measures, but must produce a "balanced" programme. Other choices include the geographical scale at which the Regulation is to be programmed, the balance of funding between different measures, and the levels of payment (within prescribed European limits) for schemes such as support for farmers in Less Favoured Areas.

- Member States can choose to implement modulation measures (which retain a proportion of direct compensation payments within Member States) for co-funding accompanying measures within the RDR.

- Member States are required to implement environmental cross-compliance measures, wherever appropriate. These make the payments of direct compensation monies to farmers conditional. However, the details of what constitutes environmental cross-compliance are left to Member State discretion.

- Member States have discretion in how they organise the spending of those resources in the new, so-called 'national envelope' under the beef regime. It is estimated that these resources will represent some £43million for the UK by 2002.

---

[1]   MAFF (1999) *Reducing Farm Subsidies – Economic Adjustment in Rural Areas*, London: Maff, p.60.

Box 9B: Measures in the Rural Development Regulation

Accompanying Measures

Agri-environment (ESAs, Countryside Stewardship, organic aid etc)

Early retirement

LFA payments (Hill Livestock Compensatory Allowances)

Afforestation of agricultural land

Non-accompanying measures

Investment in agricultural holdings

Aid for young farmers

Training

Marketing and processing grants

Other forestry

General measures promoting the development of rural areas
(see Annex A2 for full list of measures)

---

the accompanying measures and set them within a new, integrated framework in the form of a single Regulation – the Rural Development Regulation (RDR). The RDR has been hailed by the European Commission as the new 'Second Pillar' to the CAP. It combines existing accompanying measures with support for farmers in Less Favoured Areas and a range of other 'non-accompanying measures' covering farm development and wider rural development schemes (see Box 9B). The intention is that, over the longer term, as price support and compensation payments to farmers are reduced, so some of the savings can be redirected to environmental and rural development schemes through expanded use of the RDR.

9.5   The RDR will initially represent approximately 10% of CAP expenditure across the EU – though the UK has been allocated only a 3.5% share of the total (compared with, for example, Austria's 9.7% and Ireland's 7.3%). Member States are required to submit integrated Rural Development Planning Documents to the Commission by January 2000. These will

serve as Programming Documents for spending programmes under the RDR for the period 2000–2006.

Modulation

9.6   The new CAP gives Member States discretion to reduce (or 'modulate') compensation payments to farmers by up to 20% according to the labour force on the farm, its overall prosperity, and/or the total amount of aid received. These savings can then be used as additional Community support for the 'accompanying measures' within the RDR (see Box 9B). Effectively, any money used in this way becomes 'recycled' into other forms of co-financed support for agriculture. This additional support would, however, require match-funding from other domestic sources because the EU contribution is limited to a maximum of 50% (although the proportion for some measures can be up to 75% in areas designated as Objective 1).[2]

9.7   A long-term objective in the reform of the CAP is to reduce resources progressively over time from price support and

---

[2]   Objective 1 areas are those designated under the EU Structural Funds as regions with levels of GDP significantly below the EU average. In England, from next year, Merseyside, Cornwall and South Yorkshire will be designated as Objective 1 regions.

compensation payments, with some increases in resources for the RDR. Modulation offers a significant opportunity for the UK Government to redirect agricultural policy under the CAP according to its own priorities.

9.8   The arguments for applying modulation are three-fold. First, applying modulation would allow the Government to shift resources from compensation payments (which provide little or no benefit in terms of improving the competitive position of British agriculture) towards environmental and rural development measures (which assist the positive restructuring of the industry). Such a shift would improve the effective use of public resources, and increase the share of those resources targeted at achieving more desirable policy outcomes. Second, applying modulation would reduce the level of market distortions in agriculture and bring British producers closer to world market conditions, with the enhanced competitive pressures that such a move would bring. Third, a reduction in the level of direct compensation payments will enhance the relative financial attractiveness to farmers of agri-environmental schemes and so ought to widen participation. Currently, agri-environment schemes have to 'compete' with conventional agricultural systems, although conventional agriculture is artificially supported through the system of compensation payments. Any reduction in compensation payments will reduce this distortion.

9.9   Those opposed to modulation of any kind argue that: i) it risks damaging the competitive position of British farmers in the Single European Market; ii) it would be administratively complex and iii) matched-funding would be difficult to locate.

9.10 The first of these arguments rests on the belief that compensation payments help improve the competitive position of farmers. The thinking behind this belief is that if a

commodity-producing firm is faced with a loss of government subsidy and does not offset that loss by a improvement in productivity or reduction in unit cost, then its profitability will fall – and, if it is competing with firms in other countries where governments continue to provide subsidies, will face a loss of competitiveness.

9.11 But experience from other sectors suggests that reductions in subsidy do stimulate improvements in productivity and efficiency as well as encouraging a diversity of competitive strategies (indeed, this is the reason why the argument that subsidies bolster competitiveness is rarely heard outside of the agricultural sector). Often, the critical variables turn out to be the speed of change and the size of the difference between rates of subsidy: a substantial reduction in subsidy introduced at a stroke is likely to prove more detrimental to a firm's competitive position than a more gradual reduction.

9.12 However it is introduced, a reduction in the subsidy to UK agriculture is likely to take place: the long-term trajectory of CAP reform and the pattern of WTO-driven change suggest that a regime of production-related support is not sustainable and, therefore, that EU compensation payments will reduce over time. In choosing to modulate now, the UK Government would help to increase the incentives for British farmers to restructure and improve their competitive performance in advance of those Member States who choose not to modulate.

9.13 The second argument is that modulation of any kind could be administratively complex to implement. This in part arises because of the constitutional arrangements in the United Kingdom. If modulation were to be introduced, legal advice suggests it would need to be applied in a standard fashion across the UK – so any initiative in England would require the agreement of Wales,

Scotland and Northern Ireland. However, there is some flexibility in how the modulated savings can be directed within the accompanying measures, and it should be feasible for the resources to be used within the territory from which they were derived, such that national agricultural sectors within the UK are not disproportionately affected.

9.14 The third argument put forward against modulation of any kind is that the modulated savings have to be matched with 50% funding from domestic sources – and, it is argued, the provision of funds for agricultural programmes might not be viewed as a priority for the Government next to health and education.

9.15 If modulation were to be implemented in the UK, the most feasible means would be on the basis of the total amount of aid received by each farmer. The case for modulating on the basis of labour unit or overall prosperity criteria is weak. Labour unit modulation would advantage those who employ more people whether this was efficient or not, and modulation on the basis of overall prosperity criteria would be complex to administer and open to dispute over how best to judge 'prosperity'.

9.16 Even by modulating on the basis of total payments received, there are a number of options open to the Government. Two variables determine how such modulation could work. These are the level of the ceiling (or ceilings) above which payment reductions should be applied, and the rates of reduction of payments beyond

these ceilings. There are, broadly, three types of strategy open to the Government:

- "universal modulation" where all farm businesses in receipt of compensation payments would experience a single-rate reduction in them;

- "discriminatory modulation" where a ceiling is applied over a certain level of compensation payments, and so modulated receipts are taken only from larger producers; and

- "progressive modulation" where larger farm businesses would have higher proportions of their compensation payments modulated, while smaller farm businesses would be modulated at a lower rate.

9.17 The argument in favour of the latter two of these options is that they could take resources from the largest farms, which are best able to absorb a reduction in production subsidy.[3] But there are three counter-arguments:

- First, a step increase in the rate at which production payments are withdrawn after farms reach a certain size could inhibit restructuring (as well as sending a signal to the industry that the Government was more favourably disposed towards smaller rather than larger farms). Farms may be less inclined to grow through acquisition if the benefits of scale are offset by a reduction in the marginal rate of subsidy.

---

[3] However, it is not necessarily the case that, as a result of modulation, smaller farms would lose less while larger farms would lose relatively more. The savings accrued from modulation are required to be used as Community financing for accompanying measures. The resources will not leave the agricultural sector but would be refocused in line with the Government's long-term objectives for agriculture. Therefore, while there would be winners and losers, it need not necessarily be that big farmers lose and small farmers gain. Much would depend on how the modulated resources were redirected, and the size distribution of farms that might avail themselves of the new opportunities available under the expanded accompanying measures.

- Second, the options could potentially damage the UK's interests in future rounds of CAP reform. Other Member States with a smaller average farm size could argue that the thrust of the reduction in production subsidy should be borne by the larger farms in the EU (which are concentrated in the UK and Germany) – a change which, if introduced too rapidly, or on the basis of too large a differential, would harm UK farmers' international competitiveness, as well as creating potential barriers to more wide-ranging CAP reform (because other countries might see such change as a means of protecting their own, smaller farms).

- Third, the options could be difficult to administer. They could encourage attempts to evade the higher rates of modulation and could require more staff to gather the necessary information and enforce the policy. By contrast, universal modulation could be introduced quickly with little additional administrative workload.

9.18 The force of these arguments for and against progressive and discriminatory modulation varies with the rate at which larger farms' payments are modulated. If the discriminatory rate or the progressive 'step' increase for larger farms is low, then the risks to other policy objectives of inhibiting restructuring or damaging the UK's interest in Europe are low: but so is the amount of money raised. Conversely, higher rates raise more money from firms that are better able to absorb a reduction in production subsidy: but they generate more potential risks. Ultimately, while the case for modulation is strong, the case for implementing it in any form other than a single rate is more contentious and depends on a political assessment of risk and reward.

Funding modulation and wider rural development

9.19 The Government can take decisions on modulation (and on matched funding) at any time during the course of the post-Agenda 2000 financial regime, which comes into force in 2000 and runs to the end of 2006. But other decisions must be taken more quickly: in particular, the Government must submit details of how it will programme the UK's allocation of the EU budget for the RDR by January 2000. The EU allocation is smaller than many had hoped. But the way in which the Government implements the RDR will send important signals about its commitment to making use of – and, over time, expanding the size of – the CAP's 'second pillar'.

9.20 The Government also needs to consider ways of ensuring there is sufficient flexibility in UK-based budgeting systems, so that (where appropriate) budgets can be brought together from a variety of sources. The greater discretion and flexibility on agri-environment measures could be used to bring together aspects of the environmental activities of the Countryside Agency, English Nature, the National Parks and local authorities – among others – to work in partnership with the Government to provide the matched funds for the increased spending in these areas that modulation would make possible. In addition, a single pooled budget for rural development could bring together a range of activities currently funded by MAFF, DETR, a variety of agencies (including the Countryside Agency and English Nature), Regional Development Agencies and local authorities. Such a budget could create a much greater focus for rural development activities and allow a greater proportion of these to be funded in part by the EU, as well as providing greater flexibility for participating bodies.

9.21 The New Opportunities Fund currently funds health, education and environment projects in urban and rural areas and therefore makes a contribution to rural development. There may be scope to introduce explicitly rural objectives for the Fund in the future.

Farming and the environment

9.22 As far as the UK Government is concerned, part of the rationale for CAP reform has been to help improve the environmental sustainability of agriculture. There are three broad types of policy measures that can be used to help bring about a more discerning approach to countryside management and ensure the delivery of those "environmental goods" valued by the public:

- agri-environment schemes that encourage the promotion of positive environmental attributes (such as Environmentally Sensitive Areas and the Countryside Stewardship Scheme) by offering payments to farmers to maintain and improve the environment;

- more general regulatory actions (such as environmental regulation to prevent water pollution or control land development) which are designed to prohibit environmental damage;

- the application of environmental conditions to compensation payments to farmers (so-called 'cross-compliance' measures).

a) Agri-environment Schemes

9.23 Agri-environmental policy has evolved in England since the late 1970s. It was devised in response to a series of localised controversies (for example, in the Norfolk Broads and Exmoor) where farm production subsidies were fuelling the destruction of valued landscapes or habitats. The UK has led the way in developing this area of EU policy with the establishment of the first Environmentally Sensitive Areas (ESAs) in 1987. The 1992 CAP reforms introduced the 'Agri-environment Regulation'[4] as an accompanying measure to the CAP and, by 1996, 3.6% of CAP resources were spent on agri-environment schemes across the EU. Following the Agenda 2000 agreement, the resources will rise further but – unfortunately – only slightly.

9.24 In England, the agri-environment programmes (including the ESA Scheme, the Countryside Stewardship Scheme and the Organic Farming Scheme) cover a significant area: the 22 ESAs alone include over 10% of agricultural land. For most schemes, farmers sign up to a management agreement which stipulates the types of practices required to maintain and enhance the landscape, wildlife and historic value of the area by encouraging beneficial agricultural practices. On a basic level this may include restricting the use of pesticides; but there are more stringent prescriptions for some schemes (for which higher payments are offered). Different agri-environment schemes incur different levels of administrative costs. Put in broad terms, the more complex and prescriptive the scheme, the higher the costs of administration which have to be met solely by the UK Government. There is evidence that administrative efficiency improves over time.

9.25 Despite the UK's policy leadership in this area, it spends relatively little on agri-environmental schemes compared with other Member States. European Commission analysis reveals that the UK ranks 10th out of 15 in terms of the proportion of total EU expenditure allocated within the Member Stage to agri-environment schemes, and 9th in terms of the total agricultural land area under agri-environment schemes.

---

4   Regulation 2078/92.

Box 9D: The purposes of agri-environment expenditure

Agri-environment expenditure serves two main environmental purposes:-

- It helps enhance the environmental value of farming in local areas by maintaining practices which generate 'public goods' but which, in agricultural terms, are not recognised by a purely economic market mechanism.

- It provides a set of incentives for reorienting agriculture onto a more environmentally sustainable course in line with changed public priorities.

In addition, agri-environment policy also links to wider rural and regional development in the following ways:

- Countryside public goods can include not only environmental assets but also rural amenities and cultures (e.g. local land management crafts) as well as public access.

- Environmental development (such as landscape restoration, habitat creation and so on) can be an element of economic regeneration or restructuring (e.g. the creation of recreation and tourist locations).

- Countryside goods can play a key role in product and place differentiation (e.g. the Devon hedge, the Test Valley water meadows, Hadrian's Wall, Wensleydale cheese etc)[5] and the production of local distinctiveness.

9.26 In England, total expenditure on agri-environment schemes by central government amounts to around £110 million a year. The EU provides up to 50% of expenditure for these schemes, with the remainder match-funded from domestic sources. Some of the purposes and benefits of agri-environmental schemes are outlined in Box 9D.

9.27 Agri-environment programmes are popular among farmers: for example, the 1998 Countryside Stewardship scheme was significantly oversubscribed and demand for organic schemes has exhausted resources. The policy also enjoys widespread support among environmental and rural development interest groups.[6] Even the National Audit Office (NAO) has described ESAs as 'a landmark in development of policies to promote environmentally friendly farming'.[7] The NAO study concluded that the five ESA

schemes introduced in 1987 have been 'generally successful in maintaining the traditional character of the landscape and arresting environment decline'.

9.28 Evaluation evidence has shown that agri-environment schemes have been successful in conserving the environment on those farms that have entered schemes, often by preventing changes that would otherwise have been made. There is less evidence as yet (though there is some) that the schemes are actively enhancing the environment, but such enhancements will inevitably take time (e.g. nitrate leaching into ground water can take decades to reverse).

9.29 Attempts to provide economic evaluation evidence through the use of Contingent Valuation Methods (CVM) have suggested that agri-environmental schemes

[5] Centre for Rural Economy (1999) *Integrating the Environment into CAP Reform*, Newcastle University: Centre for Rural Economy.

[6] House of Commons Agriculture Committee (1997).

[7] National Audit Office (1997) *Protecting Environmentally Sensitive Areas*, London: The Stationary Office, p.2.

Table 9D – Cost-benefit analysis of agri-environmental schemes[8]

Agri-environmental scheme	Benefit estimate per person	Aggregate benefits	Scheme exchequer costs	*Net Value*	Valuation Method
Mourne Mountains and Slieve Croob ESA Moss and Chilton (1997)	Not Known	13 090 000	408 564	12 681 436	CVM
South Downs ESA Willis and Garrod (1993)	1.98-27.52	263 177*a – 79 835 000*c	970 000	(-) 707 000 – 78 865 000	CVM
Somerset levels and Moors ESA Willis and Garrod (1993)	2.45-17.53	101 422*a – 52 637 000*c	1 859 000	(-) 1 757 000 – 50 778 000	CVM
Stewartry ESA Gourlay (1995)	3.00-22.56	371 840*a – 1 825 268*b	430 000	(-) 58 160 – 1 395 268	CVM
Loch Lomond ESA Gourlay (1995)	2.28-32.8	229 600*a – 3 211 311*b	70 000 3 141 311	159 600 – CVM	CVM
Breadalbane ESA Hanley et al. (1996)	22.02-98	92 938*a – 44 100 000*c	396 796	303 858 – 43 703 204	CVM
Breadalbane ESA Hanley et al. (1996)	107.55	636 050*a – 4 841 363*b	396 796	239 251- 4 444 567	CE
Machair ESA Hanley et al. (1996)	13.4-378	75 539*a – 26 800 000*c	101 981	(-) 26 442 – 6 698 019	CVM
Machair ESA Hanley et al. (1996)	23.15	256 039*a – 563 864*b	101 981	154 058 – 461 883	CE
Norfolk Broads ESA Bateman et al. (1994)	142-150	Not Known	1 821 300	Not Known	CVM
NSA Hanley (1990)	16.17	13 506 311*e	1 500 000	12 006 311	CVM
Organic Aid Foster and Mourato (1997)	17.59	17 060 000*f	419 000	16 640 000	CR

[CVM = contingent valuation; CE = choice experiment; CR = contingent ranking. All values are in £ sterling. *a residents only. *b residents plus visitors. *c residents plus visitors plus general public. *d general public. *e East Anglia only. *f Based on saving one bird species only; aggregated over RSPB members.

[8] The Table is drawn from N. Hanley et al. (1999) *Assessing the success of agri-environmental policy in the UK*, Land Use Policy 16, 67-80, p.76. The cited references are: Bateman, I., Willis, K. & Garrod, G. (1994) *Consistency between contingent valuation estimates: a comparison of two studies of UK national parks*, Regional Studies 28 (5), 457-474; Foster, V. & Mourato, S. (1997) *Behavioural consistency, statistical specification and validity in the contingent ranking method: evidence from a survey of the impacts of pesticide use in the UK*, CSERGE Working Paper 97-09, University College London & University of East Anglia, Centre for Social and Economic Research on the Global Environment; Gourlay, D. (1995) *Loch Lomond and Stewartry ESAs: a study of public perceptions of policy benefits*. Unpublished Ph.D. Thesis, University of Aberdeen; Hanley, N. (1990) *The economics of nitrate pollution*, European Review of Agricultural Economics (17), 129-151; Moss, J &, Chilton, S. (1997) *A Socio-Economic Evaluation of the Mourne Mountains and Slieve Croob ESAs*, Queens University, Belfast, Centre for Rural Studies; Willis, K., Garrod, G. & Saunders, C. (1993) *Valuation of the South Downs and Somerset Levels ESAs*, Centre for Rural Economy, University of Newcastle-on-Tyne.

provide good value for money. The CVM studies are difficult to carry out and the results do not provide precise estimates of environmental benefits; therefore, the results of such studies need to be treated with caution. But there is now a substantial body of literature that supports their use. Table 9D summarises the findings from a large number of evaluation studies. They show the estimated ratios of net value to exchequer costs of individual agri-environment schemes as ranging from not much more than 3:1 for the Stewartry ESA to more than 260:1 for the Machair ESA.

9.30 Of course, agri-environment schemes are not the only instrument available to the Government in its pursuit of its environmental objectives. There is a need to keep in mind the validity of the 'polluter pays' principle and ensure that taxation and regulation are used wherever possible to internalise harmful externalities. But, as Chapter 6 has observed, regulation and taxation are often better suited to stopping someone doing something bad rather than encouraging them to do something good. Provided that agri-environment schemes are focused on the encouragement of positive outcomes (and are supplemented by measures to punish farmers engaged in positively harmful practices), they can serve as effective instruments. Given their value for money and popularity, there is a strong case for expanding their use.

b) Environmental Regulation

9.31 As a complement to the use of grants and payments via agri-environment programmes, the Government can protect the environment through regulation (to prevent harm) and taxation (to discourage harm). Existing regulation and environmental taxes already limit activities that harm the environment. For example, water quality has

improved through improved regulation of livestock farming practices that had previously caused pollution and imposed considerable costs on others. In addition, it would be possible to enhance the environment by increasing the coverage and impact of these policy tools, and also to review existing and future regulation to improve their quality and effectiveness, so that more can be gained with less cost and disruption to producers.

9.32 There is also a continuing debate about the role of future taxes and charges in achieving environmental improvements while also giving the agricultural industry flexibility about how to deliver them. An example of this is the concept of a pesticides tax or charge. This would seek to reduce the use of pesticides, encourage use of less harmful pesticides and increase the efficiency of usage, based on the principle that the polluter should pay. ECOTEC's recent reearch[13] estimated that a carefully designed tax or charge could result in a reduction in use of between 8% and 20%. Government should continue to consider whether such charges have a role to play in the policy mix for the agricultural industry, while also bearing in mind the scope for revenues to be recycled back into the industry, for example in reduced charges for regulation or inspection regimes.

9.33 However, there are limits to the changes in behaviour (and environmental outcomes) that can be achieved through taxation and regulation alone. For example, it is relatively easy to prevent hedgerows from being removed through regulation but much harder to bring about their reinstatement. This is where agri-environment schemes and cross-compliance (see below) come into play – by providing incentives for actions that positively improve the environment.

[13] ECOTEC (1999).

c) Cross-compliance

9.34 The so-called 'horizontal measures' of the new CAP require Member States to consider applying environmental cross-compliance conditions to compensation payments where appropriate. Some limited use has been made of cross-compliance measures in the period 1992–99. For example, the main livestock support payments to farmers can be reduced or withheld if stocking rates or management practices are deemed environmentally harmful.

9.35 The main argument in favour of cross-compliance is that it sends a strong signal to farmers that their compensation payments from the public purse are conditional on their not damaging valued rural environments. (A related argument is that, if cross-compliance is not introduced, the Government exposes itself to the risk of paying farmers to damage the environment.) In addition, for so long as the Government is required to continue with a system of production-based payments to farmers, a system of cross-compliance could be a useful means of changing the system of incentives that influence how farmers farm.[9]

9.36 There is a good case for applying cross-compliance to the spending of public money on agriculture. Environmentally irresponsible practices will, in any case, eventually undermine agriculture's own productive resources (e.g. water and soil resources, biodiversity and valued landscape resources). Cross-compliance conditions will, in effect, create a new 'regulatory floor' to help prevent the worst cases of environmental damage from agriculture.

9.37 Farming groups argue that if one Member State were to apply cross-compliance rules more enthusiastically than others, then its farmers would be placed at a competitive disadvantage. But this overlooks existing differences in national regulatory floors. In Denmark, for example, farmers are prohibited from altering many landscape features by the local planning system, and in the Netherlands detailed regulations govern the quantity of manure farmers are permitted to apply to the land.

9.38 While mindful of the need to avoid excessive constraints on farms, there is a strong case for setting a baseline for environmental standards for UK agriculture. The current Codes of Good Agricultural Practice[10] provide guidance which could be used as the starting point for drawing up cross-compliance conditions.

9.39 This regulatory floor would need to be reviewed from time to time, to take account of changes in economic, social and environmental circumstances. For example, it could include strengthening the protection of landscape features and existing farm habitats from destruction, which is a current requirement of ESA Tier 1 agreements. However, to the extent that these provisions currently contribute to the calculation of ESA payment rates, this change would imply a net reduction in ESA receipts and would require the raising the environmental baseline of all ESA Tier 1 prescriptions (in Statutory Instruments) and individual management agreements.

9.40 Cross-compliance measures would need to be implemented rigorously, otherwise there is a risk that they may be flouted. Monitoring of compliance with environmental conditions would require some degree of expertise (as is the case now). However, some of the simpler conditions (e.g. the presence or absence

---

[9] Baldock, D & Mitchell, K. (1995) *Cross-Compliance Within the Common Agricultural Policy*, London: Institute for European Environmental Policy.

[10] These Codes cover air, soil, water, the use of pesticides, and the application of nitrogen in Nitrate Vulnerable Zones; and there is a draft code for conservation in preparation.

of features) could be achieved through the current system of routine Integrated Administration and Control Systems (IACS) inspections, which combine remote sensing by satellite, air photographs and field visits. Monitoring would nevertheless have some resource implications. These would need to be considered carefully when designing an approach to implementation.

The future of support for hill farmers

9.41 The UK has a long tradition of providing additional support to hill farmers because they farm in physically harsh conditions but provide valuable land management services in some of the nation's most spectacular upland landscapes. Since 1975, this support has principally been in the form of Hill Livestock Compensation Allowances (HLCAs), paid on a headage basis, in Less Favoured Areas (LFAs).[11]

9.42 Hill farm incomes have remained low compared to other sectors in recent years with the result that some LFA producers have left the industry and those remaining have become increasingly dependent upon subsidies. It is not uncommon for subsidies to represent more than 100% of net farm income with the bulk of the support coming through the sheep and beef regimes. The impact of market forces means that further restructuring is likely.

9.43 The Agenda 2000 reforms mean that two key changes must be made to LFA support. First, compensatory allowances must be paid on an area basis rather than according to headage (i.e. payments per hectare will replace payments per animal). Second, the support will have a stronger environmental

objective since payments will be conditional on the use of "usual good farming practices, compatible with the need to safeguard the environment and maintain the countryside, in particular by sustainable farming"[12].

9.44 These new arrangements are likely to involve some redistribution of support away from more densely stocked holdings and in favour of those with lower stocking rates. Given that the number of sheep in the LFAs has increased significantly over the last 15 years, removing the headage basis for LFA payments (which, together with the Sheep Annual Premium, served as an incentive to increase stocking densities on often fragile upland grazings) is a welcome first step.

9.45 LFA support will have to be refocused along the lines already laid out in the CAP reforms. In England, payments should continue to be focussed on livestock producers (beef and sheep) rather than other agricultural sectors[13]. Environmental conditions should be applied over and above what is currently the minimum standard or the standards required by the new cross-compliance arrangements.

9.46 Further refocusing of policy would shift the rationale for extra payments to hill farmers away from simply maintaining a farming population in the hills and towards supporting farmers for the land management and environmental services they provide. Ultimately, the Government could aim for a system in which all additional LFA support in England would be wholly conditional on farmers' participation in agri-environment management agreements. This approach fits with the Government's wider priorities for public spending which seek to tie public expenditure to improvements in policy outcomes.[14]

[11] LFAs cover all the main hill areas of the UK. While about half of the UK's total agricultural area is designated, the proportion is just 12% in England, and centres on the Northern Uplands and south west regions.

[12] Article 14 of Council Regulation 1257/1999.

[13] There is a small amount of dairy farming in the LFAs.

[14] Chief Secretary to the Treasury (1998) *Public Services for the Future: Modernisation, Reform, Accountability – Comprehensive Spending Review Public Service Agreements 1999-2002*, Cm4181, London: HMSO.

9.47 Such an approach could be applied to England only. Visits to Scotland, Wales & Northern Ireland revealed somewhat different policy priorities for hill farmers, because of different socio-economic and physical conditions. Among the component parts of the UK, the balance of arguments between social priorities and environmental priorities inevitably varies. It follows that, from 2000 onwards, LFA policy should be programmed and administered in a devolved way which reflects the different natural, social and economic conditions in each of the devolved administrations.

Competitive strategies for farming

9.48 The Government has produced a strategy for the future development of the agricultural sector. The strategy is driven by the continuing pressure for restructuring faced by all sectors of the industry.

9.49 The agricultural sector will need to continue to restructure in response to changing economic pressures, and some farms will grow larger while some farmers will exit the industry. However, farm businesses will also need to develop new ways to respond to the competitive challenges of the future. A series of competitive strategies can be identified above and beyond competing solely in terms of low cost. These strategies are unlikely ever wholly to replace a focus on cost reduction. But they can be invaluable supplementary strategies. They are:

- adding value to products;

- developing more direct links with consumers;

- collaborative efforts with other producers, suppliers, processors and retailers;

- diversification of farm-based activities;

- adopting new technologies;

- developing non-food crops.

a) Adding Value to Products

9.50 Many farm businesses could increase competitiveness by adding value to farm products. Options include:

- enhancing the quality of the end-product and so securing a premium on the price;

- differentiating products on the basis of the type of production (e.g. organic farming, environment and/or animal-friendly farming, or other quality assurance schemes);

- differentiating products on the basis of local heritage and distinctiveness (many food products contain local ingredients, and are produced using local methods, breeds or varieties. Examples would include Scottish beef, Cumberland sausages, Cornish clotted cream or locally-branded cheeses);

- incorporating further processing of food products on the farm site (such as processing milk into butter or cheese, for example), or developing new or improved products and processing techniques.

9.51 The extent to which these options are pursued is a matter for individual businesses. But, apart from exhortation and encouragement, the Government could assist in two ways. First, working through MAFF and the RDAs, it could encourage farms to register regional and traditional food and drink names under the EU 'Protected Food Names Scheme' and support local-branding initiatives where these will help businesses to market their products more effectively. Second, it could help farmers to take advantage of the considerable scope for innovation in the development of new markets and the development and application of new or improved products and processing techniques (including the development of technologies for the traceability of food products) through the provision of grant aid. Grants are currently available in all parts of the UK except England for co-ordinating efforts, facilitating the development of new markets, supporting capital investment for agricultural processing and marketing, and providing advice to small producers and marketing co-operatives. Such grants could form part of the Government's programmes for implementing the Rural Development Regulation in England.

9.52 Perhaps the best-known example of differentiation by method of production is organic food. The main components of organic farming systems are the avoidance of manufactured fertilisers and pesticides and, in their place, the use of crop rotation and other forms of husbandry to maintain soil fertility and control pests. The principal argument for government support of organic farming relates to the method's environmental benefits; but there are other market failures that government intervention might address. Domestic production of organic food is lagging behind demand – it is estimated that around three quarters of the organic food consumed in the UK is imported. Conversion can take up to five years of using organic techniques (while the effects of previous non-organic production are allowed to diminish), before the output can be described as "organic". The length of this transition can be a disincentive to change. Moreover, it is expensive – the lower productivity of organic methods (and the production subsidies foregone) are not offset by the premium that organic products command. While in theory these transition costs could be met by borrowing, the market may in practice find it difficult to meet this need. This is for a combination of reasons:

- farm businesses may not have sufficient resources to fund the transition from their own reserves;

- commercial lenders may be wary to lend what are often relatively large sums to relatively small businesses;

- commercial lenders may be too short-term in their lending perspectives (they are discouraged by the length of the transition);

- commercial lenders may be too risk-averse in the face of a relatively new market (organics) which is growing rapidly (they are discouraged by the uncertainty over the size and durability of the premium for organic products).

9.53 One response to the market failure would be to provide more information to allow commercial lenders to price this borrowing more accurately. However, the key information is a longer time-series of data on the organics market and more evidence of the time and costs of conversion – information that, at this stage of the market's development, is not available. Thus there is a case for time-limited support for conversion to organics: to offset the extra costs of conversion created by the CAP subsidies foregone, and to help provide this information.

9.54 During 1997/98 the Government reviewed support for organic farming. The Review found that the UK was 15th out of 22 European countries surveyed in terms of utilisable area certified as organic or in conversion in 1996/97 (See Annex A4). Because relatively few farmers were converting to organic farming, payment rates were revised upwards. In April 1999 MAFF launched its new Organic Farming Scheme to enhance the incentives for those farmers who wish to convert to organic production. The budget for the new Scheme is some £6.2million for 1999/00 and represents approximately a doubling of support. The new Scheme is totally committed this year. There is, therefore, a case for further strengthening the Organic Farming Scheme in order to expand participation. In considering further expansion of the Organic Farming Scheme, the Government should focus on the (time-limited) conversion to organic production, rather an open-ended system of income maintenance payments; and the scheme should be closely monitored to ensure that it continues to represent value for money.

b) Developing More Direct Links with Consumers

9.55 A further competitive approach for farmers is to increase the sector's influence over the distribution and retail of food products. One recent example of such a strategy that has attracted much attention has been the establishment of Farmers' Markets. Since 1997, Farmers' Markets have been established in a number of towns and cities, including Bath, Bristol, London and Lewes.

The emphasis is on the provision of local food produce. The markets have the additional benefit of creating new opportunities for direct dialogue between producers and consumers which, in turn, increases consumers' understanding of production methods and farmers' understanding of consumers' preferences (see Box 9E).

9.56 The National Association of Farmers' Markets estimates that the total number of markets will exceed 50 by the year 2000. There is a suggestion, however, that the establishment and expansion of some markets is being inhibited by local market charter arrangements (many date back to the Middle Ages). A market charter establishes the right to set up a market on a particular site and prohibits the establishment of any other markets within six and two-thirds miles (the

Box 9E: Case Study: Hampshire Farmers' Markets pilot

The aim of Hampshire Farmers' Markets is to provide an outlet for local produce and to enable local consumers to make direct contact with producers. They can help environmental sustainability by encouraging organic production, reducing transportation miles, packaging and waste, as well as supporting agricultural diversification.

Three pilot farmers' markets in Winchester were planned for 1999; two have already taken place at the time of writing. Preliminary indications are extremely positive. On both occasions the average takings per farmer has been about £500.

Date	No of visitors	Turnover (est. £000)
May 16th	7,500	15–20
July 4th	10,000	25–30

Each farmer pays £20 to hire a stall for the day from the City Council, which also provides the location. The success of the first pilot (which attracted 30 farmers and growers) led to greater interest for the second (which attracted 49 farmers and growers). The September market has attracted 53 farmers.

In addition, Farmers' Markets could give a welcome boost to town and city centre locations – retailers in Winchester report takings up 30% for the time of year. Part of the success has been attributed to the positive and proactive role adopted by the County Council and Local Authority. They have worked in partnership with the National Farmers' Union and private businesses to get the scheme off the ground. If the analysis of the pilots proves them to have been a success the County Council aims to extend the scheme across Hampshire.

distance once considered as practical to travel to and from by horse in one day). This anachronistic legislation means farmers' markets generally cannot be established without the agreement of any local charter market. There would be merit in reviewing this legislation and accompanying regulations.

c) Collaborative Efforts with Other Producers, Suppliers, Processors and Retailers

9.57 Collaboration is another means by which farm businesses can improve their competitive position. Collaboration can be horizontal (i.e. among primary producers) or vertical (i.e. between primary producers and suppliers, processor or retailers).

9.58 Collaborative marketing is one way for producers to secure professional marketing expertise, technical support and savings on input costs. Additional benefits include increased scale, quality control and continuity of supply. In comparison with the rest of continental Europe, Britain does not have a strong tradition of collaboration.[15] However, there has been a recent increase in such activities in response to competitive pressures in the industry. There are plenty of opportunities for further growth and development of farmer controlled businesses in the UK. Grant aid for marketing and processing is also permitted by the EU under the RDR.

d) Diversification of Farm-Based Activities

9.59 The diversification of farm household incomes has been taking place for much of the past two decades. It is important to draw a distinction between 'on-farm' and 'off-farm' diversification. The former includes farm shops and food processing or tourism and recreation enterprises. The latter involves off-farm employment by farmers or members of farming families. Surveys have consistently shown that the latter is of greater significance.

9.60 Farm income evidence for 1997/98 published by MAFF stated that 60% of full time farms have some form of off-farm income and that the average income generated was £5,000 per annum. One national study of the extent of on-farm diversification was conducted in the early 1990s by researchers at Exeter University.[16] The research found that over 40 per cent of surveyed farms had at least one non-farming enterprise. Overall, the study estimated that diversification contributed something in the order of £230million to the income (net margin) on all agricultural holdings in England and Wales; contributing some 11 per cent to total business income. This proportion is likely to have grown since the survey was conducted, because farm incomes are now slightly lower than in 1990. The provision of leisure-related (accommodation and recreation) services was uniformly the most common form of diversification, followed by the supply of machinery contracting services, adding value to farm produced products, producing speciality products and miscellaneous services, in that order. MAFF collects some data on farm diversification annually as part of the Farm Business Survey. Policy-making could be usefully informed by updating the national survey on diversification.

e) Adopting New Technologies

9.61 A recent study of the routes to prosperity for UK agriculture produced by the National Farmers' Union highlighted the likely impact of technological change upon farming in the next century. These include the extension of IT into the farm business as an aid to administration and management planning and day-to-day operation; and the application of IT and precision farming techniques to improve the accuracy and efficacy of crop inputs. There is also the

[15] NFU (1999) Routes to Prosperity for UK Agriculture, London: NFU, p.20 & p.27.

[16] J. McInerney & M. Turner (1991) Patterns, Performance and Prospects in Farm Diversification, Agricultural Economics Unit: Exeter University.

continuing application of plant breeding techniques, for example to improve crop yields and limit the need for applications of fertilisers and pesticides; this also includes new bioscience developments, including the current programme of trials of genetically modified crops to see whether, in the future, GM crops could be grown safely in the UK commercially.

9.62 The first of these in particular links to the issue of improved ICT application in rural areas; and both link to proposals form improved support for skills and training for people living and working in the countryside, and especially the proposals for enhanced rural business qualifications and provision through the University for Industry and other providers. Both of these are explained in more detail in Chapter 7.

f) Non-Food Crops

9.63 Continuing technological, market and regulatory changes are likely to continue to alter the relative economic costs and benefits to farms of diversifying into non-food crops. Recent years have seen increasing interest in the potential for energy crops as an alternative use for agricultural land. Government policy, through England's forestry strategy, is to support a targeted programme for short-rotation coppice planting and encourage the use of wood fuel for energy production using the most efficient technologies. Expanding the area of renewable energy crops grown would also assist in the meeting of the UK's international obligation on climate change and the reduction of greenhouse gas emissions.

9.64 The Government's current forestry policy is for a continued steady expansion of the woodland area,[19] and provisions are made for support for the afforestation of agricultural land under the Rural Development Regulation. The development of forestry can assist in the development of rural economies. The last employment survey carried out by the Forestry Commission showed that some 19,000 people worked in the forestry and wood-processing sector in England.[20] Additional benefits can accrue from the environmental and recreational contribution of forestry development, and forestry is increasingly being seen as a means of economic regeneration of some former industrial land sites. The viability of forestry is, however, related to the CAP, and as CAP reform lowers land values over the longer term, forestry will become comparatively more competitive.

Procedures for change

a) Programming the Rural Development Regulation

9.65 The RDR specifies that "Rural development plans shall be drawn up at the geographical level deemed to be the most appropriate".[21] This leaves it entirely to the Member States to decide on the appropriate internal level for implementation. Thus, programming could be at the national level if states chose to do so, although this would not be in the spirit of the decentralised approach the Commission is promoting.

9.66 MAFF has consulted a wide range of interests on how the Rural Development Regulation should best be implemented and, in particular, on the geographical level at which Rural Development Plans should be drawn up, and who should be involved in their preparation and implementation. As a result, MAFF has announced how it will take forward rural development programming to enable the submission of plans within the

[19] Forestry Commission (1999) *A New Focus for England's Woodlands: Strategic Priorities and Programmes*, Cambridge: Forestry Commission.

[20] Forestry Commission, 1994.

[21] Article 41, para 1.

European Commission's deadline of the end of 1999. There will be a Rural Development Plan for England comprising a national framework document with nine regional chapters or plans, based on Government Office regions.

9.67 Member States must include agri-environment measures throughout their territories and "ensure the necessary balance" is kept between the other measures contained in the Regulation (Article 43(2)). The guidance says "emphasis must be on participation and a 'bottom up' approach".

9.68 In the UK, the agricultural structure funds (including all the existing farm development measures that will be absorbed into the RDR) have very largely been administered by the agriculture departments and usually applied to farm-based diversification. On the other hand, rural development funds (mainly from domestic sources) have been administered by regional and national agencies. At present, the agriculture departments, Forestry Commission and Intervention Board are the only government bodies which have the necessary accreditation from the European Commission to make the CAP-funded payments under the RDR, and the Commission has indicated that it does not wish to extend accreditation directly to any new bodies.

9.69 In developing and implementing the rural development plans, MAFF will increasingly be operating within the context of the Government's regional agenda, and the work of the new Regional Development Agencies (RDAs). The RDAs will be required to draw up regional economic strategies for their territories, including the rural areas, and the preparation of programmes under the RDR will need to be sufficiently integrated with the work and responsibilities of the new

RDAs. (Indeed, Article 39 of the RDR requires that compatibility and consistency be ensured.)

9.70 In order to improve co-ordination and foster an integrated approach to rural and agricultural policy, MAFF and the Farming and Rural Conservation Agency, the RDAs and Government Regional Offices, English Nature and the Countryside Agency, and other national and regional partners, should continue to work together on rural development planning. This process should generate integrated regional strategies for agricultural and rural development in the English regions, and would result in input from a wide range of bodies with an interest in rural development feeding into the Rural Development Regulation.

b) The UK Government's Strategy for Further CAP Reform

9.71 The UK Government's objectives for the CAP have been to bring about through negotiation, an EU agricultural policy which:

- reduces costs to consumers whilst safeguarding the quality and safety of food;

- reduces the level of taxpayer support for farming;

- encourages the development of farm businesses and farm structures able to compete in growing world markets without on-going subsidy;

- facilitates EU enlargement;

- stimulates innovation and research;

- fosters environmentally sound agricultural practices;

- encourages sustainable rural development.[22]

9.72 Agenda 2000 continued the process of CAP reform that began in the 1980s. In effect, the EU has agreed a new vision for

[22] Minister of Agriculture's Agricultural Advisory Group (1999) *Europe's Agriculture – The Case for Change*, London: MAFF, p.25.

agriculture and for intervention in rural areas, to be implemented through changes to production support and the use of the CAP's 'second pillar' – the Rural Development Regulation.

9.73 It is disappointing that the Agenda 2000 reforms were not as fundamental as the UK Government had hoped for. In particular, the agreed limits on CAP expenditure for 2000–2006 show overall growth in real terms. Additional expenditure arises from compensation payments to producers and this more than offsets the budgetary savings which arise from the reductions in support prices. One of the most effective ways of reducing the level of taxpayer support for farming will be through future reform of the system of compensation payments.

9.74 There is a concern that the current CAP deal will not be politically and economically sustainable for the duration of the intended financial perspective (2000–2006). The World Trade Organisation is due to open talks on international agricultural trade under the Uruguay Round Agreement of the GATT at the end of 1999 and the existing CAP arrangements include subsidies that are incompatible with WTO rules. The Uruguay round included a 'Peace Deal' that prevented challenge of the CAP, but this expires in 2003. In addition, there remain questions over the timetable for EU enlargement to embrace new Member States in Eastern Europe and the arrangements for their entry into the CAP. Taken together, it is possible that the CAP reforms will have to be re-opened at some stage before 2006. This would open an opportunity for the UK to take forward its negotiating strategy for long-term CAP reform.

9.75 The UK strategy for pressing the case for further CAP reform should be informed by a clear vision of the following long-term aims:

- to phase out price support and compensation payments at the earliest practicable opportunity;

- to provide funding to the agricultural sector in the longer term for public goods (eg certain environmental goods) where necessary and justified; and

- to manage change through transitional rural restructuring programmes, funded by the RDR.

9.76 Further EU reform will be more effectively pursued if the UK is able to:

- continue to take a lead in promoting the case for change among EU partners;

- articulate a vision of a competitive, forward-looking and modernised agriculture in England with multiple outputs;

- actively participate in current discretionary opportunities for reform (such as those associated with the RDR and the horizontal measures);

- build and broaden alliances among other current and future Member States, especially those in southern and central Europe.

9.77 A central part of this case should be the progressive reduction in compensation payments, with a proportion of the savings being redirected towards the CAP's Second Pillar and its wider rural development and agri-environmental objectives. Such an approach has the strategic advantage of avoiding the false choice between the 'scrap the CAP' approach of the policy's most vociferous critics in the UK and the approach of those who wish to maintain subsidy payments at their current levels in perpetuity. The Government has the opportunity to 'lead by example' in this approach by making use of the opportunities to begin reorienting the CAP towards its own longer term objectives.

10. FORGING A NEW COMMITMENT TO RURAL COMMUNITIES

Summary

Persistent poverty and social exclusion, a declining number of service outlets and a reliance on private transport create challenges for the Government to ensure that rural communities are equipped to take advantage of economic opportunities. A new commitment to rural communities from government will require:

- Innovative approaches to service delivery;

- A new role for market towns as the key centres for much economic activity and service delivery in rural areas;

- Improved access to public, private, commercial and voluntary transport; and

- Recognition of the importance of affordable and social housing in achieving the Government's economic, environmental and social objectives for rural England.

Services need to be brought closer to people through joined-up provision, shared facilities, and more rational provision, including recognition of the key role played by market towns. Access will also depend on integrating transport and making the car affordable and accessible to more people. Communities also need to have affordable housing to buy or rent.

A new commitment to rural communities

10.1 Rural communities remain, by and large, strong and vibrant. But they are not immune from the social and economic challenges facing the country as a whole. Problems of access to services, poverty, and social exclusion all exist in the countryside, not only in more remote or sparsely populated areas, or those where industries such as mining are in decline, but even in seemingly prosperous districts. These problems could worsen if the implications of economic, social and technological change are ignored. But if these changes are recognised and even harnessed, the result could be real improvements in services for rural areas, and a better quality of life for country people.

10.2   Strengthening all communities, and tackling the problems of social exclusion, cannot be left to the market. A new approach is needed which recognises the real problems facing rural communities, the importance of promoting rural economies, and the need to take account of local circumstances. This approach should include:

- innovative approaches to the provision of services in villages and market towns;

- a key role for market towns as the economic nodes for the delivery of rural services;

- better accessibility, especially to market towns, to gain access to rural services and jobs; and

- access to social and affordable housing.

10.3   Strategies would need to be developed at the regional and local level to achieve this. The Government Offices (including MAFF's regional presence) are probably best placed to co-ordinate this at the regional level working closely with local authorities, the Countryside Agency and the RDAs. But implementation would need to be at the local level, with the focus on local services and being driven by local needs and circumstances. Rural local authorities should liaise with local communities, the Rural Community Councils and Parish councils, in mapping out what services are available and in developing local strategies for delivering services. As far as possible, existing mechanisms should be used for developing strategies. Rural local authorities' community plans may be one way of developing strategies for rural services.

Innovative approaches to delivering rural services

10.4   There are a number of innovative approaches which can bolster the viability of rural services. The most appropriate mix will vary depending upon the type of service and local circumstances.

a) *Joining up and delivering services*

10.5   Joined-up service delivery offers one of the most promising avenues for retaining and enhancing rural services. Services such as the village shop and the post office are often already combined, but other links are possible. For instance, banking services could be provided through the post office or public services through the village hall. The scale economies, synergies and additional income created by combining one service with another, allow services to be provided where they would otherwise be uneconomic. Thus existing services can be retained or new services introduced. The combination of services can also provide an additional focus for the community, with wider social benefits including building social capital. The impetus for joining up services often comes from community action (the barriers to which are discussed in more detail later in this chapter). Box 10A provides one case study taken from a growing pool of examples.

10.6   At present there is no dedicated national programme to encourage the joining up of services. Such a programme could include:

- providing information and business advice about opportunities and best practice;

- giving guidance and advice on complying with any hurdles e.g planning or legal constraints;

- giving loans or grants to meet appraisal or feasibility study costs or help with set up costs; and

Box 10A: Joint provision of services

- **Cockfield, Co. Durham** – in 1997/98 RDC gave a £7,000 grant as 25% of the cost of upgrading the Community Centre to provide: a permanent community police office; subsidised meals for the elderly; disabled access and an induction loop for the hard of hearing; a youth club; a veterinary surgery; chiropody services; prescription collection; multimedia and ICT facilities.

- working with the public, voluntary and private sector to establish links and match up services.

10.7 Such a programme would be useful in identifying new opportunities, and undertaking trials of innovative approaches to joined-up service delivery, with significant wider economic and social benefits. The Countryside Agency may be best placed to take forward such a programme.

10.8 While rural-specific programmes have an important role to play in the provision of public services, it is also true that mainstream public spending (on health, education, employment, law and order, social security, etc.) is still the most important source of funding for public services in rural areas.

10.9 Departments involved in the delivery of services in rural areas should explore the scope for joint service delivery, as part of the next Spending Review. This could provide significant synergies that would allow a greater range of services to be delivered in local areas. It is likely to be particularly relevant to market towns, which should be key centres for the joint delivery of services to rural community.

10.10 Many key public services are provided by local authorities. Local authorities will also need to review joining up delivery of their own services, within their local service delivery strategies. There are already good examples of this happening in urban areas, such as one-stop-shops in Lewisham for income support and housing benefits and in Camden which combine income support,

child support and housing and council tax benefit. Government Offices should liaise with local authorities to explore the scope for delivering both central and local government services to rural communities at shared sites and for joining up funding streams.

10.11 In taking decisions about closures of public services in rural areas, Government Departments need to consider the ramifications not just for the achievement of their own objectives but for the Government's objectives as a whole. In many cases, rationalising service provision will bring overall benefits, but Departments need to be more alert to circumstances where this will not be the case. For example, rationalisation, where it increases distances that people have to travel to reach a service, transfers costs from the delivery organisation to the rural population. Therefore, the wider costs and benefits of changes in public services, including external costs such as travel times, should be assessed. This would be consistent with the appraisal of new public sector investments.

10.12 Within public expenditure, there has been a shift in policy towards the use of area-based programmes to target particular concentrations of disadvantage (ill-health, under-achievement, long-term unemployment, etc.). Zone-based initiatives – Health Action Zones (HAZs), Education Action Zones (EAZs), Employment Zones (EZs) among others – illustrate this trend. Arguably, the problems of diffuse services, sparse population and lack of access mean that a zone-based approach – addressing, co-ordinating and organising the service provision across the zone – can offer a potent solution in rural areas.

10.13 The concern that this zone-based approach raises is that it can be easy to focus on the problems of inner cities and urban areas. Policymakers may overlook the problems of a similar weight in some rural areas (though the problems in rural areas are often more dispersed, and are therefore less visible in statistics at the local authority district level). This can result in rural areas missing out.

10.14 Taking employment as an example, none of the ten English EZs covers a rural area. Yet there are five rural districts among the 50 Local Authority districts with the highest long-term unemployment in England, and four of these have unemployment rates of over 10%[1] (out of 47 English districts with unemployment over 10%) . And either unemployment or long term unemployment is worse in these rural districts than in three of the ten EZ areas. Moreover, the targeted EZ approach offers the prospect of real improvements in rural areas where unemployment is often concentrated in relatively small pockets and where incremental employment growth in the surrounding economy is insufficient on its own to address the problem. The picture is better on health, where five out of 26 HAZs cover rural areas. One good-practice example is the North Cumbria HAZ, which includes £160,000 of expenditure in 1999/00 on innovative services for people living in rural areas. And for education, while only two out of 25 EAZs cover rural areas, at least seven out of 47 potential EAZs shortlisted for the second round of zones have a rural flavour, so there is scope for improving coverage.

10.15 Other recent initiatives also offer the opportunity to address the problems of rural areas. For example, NHS Direct, the new NHS telephone helpline, will provide access to information and advice about health and the NHS 24 hours a day, seven days a week for the entire population of England, not just those in urban areas. And NHS walk-in centres (the first wave of which were announced by the Prime Minister in April 1999, with a further 17 announced by the Secretary of State for Health in September) offer improved access for people who live in rural areas (with limited primary health provision) but work or shop in towns and larger urban settlements. Similarly, the 800 IT learning centres announced by the Secretary of State for Education in March[2], offer potentially important access to ICT in rural areas, which has much to offer for rural service provision.

10.16 There is some evidence[3] that for a number of services, such as education, social services, public transport and police, rural areas have lower spending per head than urban areas. This disparity would be compounded by the, often, higher cost of delivering some rural services. However, such comparisons are beset with problems. The quantity and type of services that need to be delivered can vary greatly and determining the allocation of resources across different tiers of Government is extremely difficult. At the same time, significant support is being given to rural areas. For example, because of universal service obligations for utilities such as telephones, gas, electricity and water and sewerage and funding arrangements for Post Offices, many rural dwellers obtain significant cross-subsidies from urban counterparts.

---

[1] NOMIS (March – May 1998), *Labour Force Survey.*

[2] Department for Education and Employment (1999), Press Notice 113/99, "£400 million to bridge the gap between the computer haves and have nots".

[3] For example, the DTZ Pieda report commissioned by the Countryside Agency and as yet unpublished '*Public Expenditure in Rural Areas*' and the RDC paper (1996 RRR No 22) '*Fair shares for rural areas*'.

10.17 The Government is currently undertaking a large-scale review of arrangements for thje financing of local government. This review includes an evaluation of the Standard Spending Assessment (SSA) mechanism, which determines the allocation of funds to local authorities. The SSA review should consider whether rural areas are fairly treated and whether sufficient weight is attached to the effect of population sparsity and dispersed settlement patterns on the costs of service delivery.

b) *Mobile and shared service provision*

10.18 Mobile provision of services, such as peripatetic GP surgeries, is one way of keeping some access to services within rural areas. Rotating provision between a number of fixed sites, e.g. for a day a week at each site, as well as transporting facilities around in a trailer, may be a cost-effective means of providing key services. This approach is being used successfully by the Employment Service in some rural areas. For some services, such as small village schools or day care centres, small size makes it difficult to support management overheads. Economies of scale can be achieved by grouping a number of units under a single management structure. To take one example: a 'clustering' approach has been successful for a group of Dorset village schools which shared the headteacher and management functions across several schools. Departments and agencies might be encouraged to examine more mobile and part-time delivery of services as part of a wider review of rural service provision.

c) *Community enterprise and action*

10.19 The involvement of the local community is often a key ingredient in the retention or improvement of rural services. Community involvement is also important as part of the wider process of building local partnerships and social capital and providing an input into planning process and development strategies. The local community can reach an agreed view of what services are needed and are likely to be viable (this may include carrying out a village appraisal as discussed in Chapter 8); raise funds locally; apply for the grants or loans for rural projects; find ways to combine services e.g. within village halls; or provide services through operating as a community enterprise such as a friendly society, co-operative or credit union.

10.20 Support is available to communities from, among others, the Countryside Agency, Rural Community Councils, Regional Development Agencies, Action with Communities in Rural England (the national association of Rural community councils, a charity which helps the development of diverse and sustainable rural communities), Village Retail Services Association (a charity which provides a national body to support village shops), local councils, the Post Office and private trusts. Box 10B gives two examples of successful initiatives.

10.21 There is scope for more community action of this kind but it faces a number of perceived and actual constraints:

- town and country planning and environmental health legislation are seen by some as inhibiting action (though a 1997 RDC report on the joint provision of rural services[4] found little evidence of this);

- charity law means that for a post office to be located in a village hall, the accommodation to be used must be declared as surplus to requirements; have a market rent calculated; and have a lease drawn up;

- child safety legislation limits other uses of schools for the benefit of rural communities;

---

4   RDC (1997), 'The joint provision of rural services', Rural Research Report number 34.

Box 10B: Community Action In Operation

Upton Grey, Hampshire – Following the closure of the village shop in 1996, a campaign raised £100,000 to extend and alter the village hall. More than half this money came from local residents, the rest was made up of grants from local and county councils, the National Lottery and the RDC. The new hall incorporates a village shop and post office. Other improvements include a toilet, disabled access and an induction loop for the hard of hearing, energy efficient lighting storage space and a PA system.

Tytherington, Gloucestershire – The village shop closed in June 1996. A village shop association was formed as a friendly society to raise funds to build a new one. One of the methods used was villagers purchasing £50 bonds. £20,000 was raised and the shop and Post Office re-opened in May 1998. It is run on a voluntary basis.

- licensing laws are seen as inhibiting additional uses of pubs – however, this appears to arise from magistrates' use of their discretionary powers, rather than provisions in licensing laws;

- the implications of business rates may discourage commercial uses of charitable premises; and

- managers of voluntary schemes need to devote an extensive amount of time to funding applications, especially where funding is from multiple sources with different criteria and timescales.

10.22 Working within these constraints requires dynamism to overcome planning constraints, raise funding, ensure charity law is not breached etc. There are ways round some of these problems:

- if planning permission is needed a parish council can apply for it at half the fee of other organisations;

- where there is only one shop or post office in a settlement of under 3,000 in a designated area and its rateable value is under £5,000, it receives 50% rate relief and, at the discretion of the council, it can receive 100% relief. Councils also have discretion to extend this provision to shops or post offices with a rateable value of up to £10,000;

- the RDC had a successful programme to support Village Halls which is now being progressed by the Countryside Agency. Parish councils have powers to provide financial support for both post offices and village halls;

- Post office guidance on ways of placing post offices within village halls needs to be more widely promulgated. The post office also runs a community office scheme, with revenue payments weighted towards hours of opening rather than the volume of business; and

- the Home Office review of licensing law should consider whether there are any ways in which magistrates can be encouraged to look favourably on the joint provision of services within village pubs, where this is appropriate.

10.23 There is a need for further work to consider developing a 'community chest' scheme to help fund innovative local community action, support initiatives to develop rural services and develop participatory processes such as village appraisals.

d) *Information and Communication Technology in rural areas*

10.24 Future developments in Information and Communication Technology (ICT) are potentially a key means of delivering services and work opportunities. Rural areas face three main barriers to exploiting the opportunities:

- lack of broadband telecommunications infrastructure in rural areas, which allows access to high capacity data transfer (such as video calls);

- lack of awareness of the opportunities offered by ICT; and

- low take-up of access to the Internet.

10.25 Infrastructure issues are discussed in Chapter 7. A NERA report for the Rural Development Commission[5] identified lower awareness of advanced ICT services in rural areas (33% of residents were aware of advanced ICT services compared to 40% in urban areas) and a slightly lower take-up of these services (3% in rural areas compared to 4% in urban areas). This may partly reflect the lower take-up of advanced ICT by rural businesses. There is also a risk that some households in rural areas will suffer from ICT exclusion as the use of ICT and E-commerce becomes more important.

10.26 These problems might be tackled through the establishment of information hubs in rural settlements. These could be centred on local post offices or other local amenities such as schools or community centres. They would deliver a range of services such as electronic Government, banking, local public-transport information, on-line health advice, training and education, teleshopping and ordering of library books (possibly with collection from a local access point). There are synergies between greater use of ICT and joining up service delivery. In market towns, for example, tourist and local information centres and libraries could be brought together and boosted by the use of ICT. More generally, market towns could provide staffed sites that offered detailed advice and information on government services and the use of ICT facilities. Video links could then be provided to the local access points in smaller villages. In time, organisations would be able to bid for the franchise to run such access points, but the first step would be to pilot these proposals. Some people's reluctance to use some forms of ICT instead of face-to-face contact will need to be considered. However, by strengthening the role of post offices or other local access points, the scheme could facilitate more social interaction, and help to overcome some of the difficulties of gaining information about public transport services in rural areas (see section on transport later in this chapter).

10.27 Teleshopping has the potential to expand the range of goods and services that village shops, post offices and other outlets can offer in rural areas, where these can serve as ordering points as well as collection points. Of course, if teleshopping is entirely by home-based Internet or digital-TV access with deliveries to the door, this could have significant implications for the pattern of rural services.

10.28 ICT and telephone call centres could also play a role in co-ordinating transport services, such as public and voluntary transport, car sharing schemes and taxi services. These could take journey details, work out several journey plans and cost options and then allow customers to decide how they wished to travel. This could be piloted at a regional level or with a number of counties.

10.29 Teleworking, where employees work at home using IT links to their HQ, also offers significant potential benefits, by retaining more employment within rural communities. There is

5 RDC (1999) *Access to bandwidth, implications for rural areas*, National Economic Research Associates.

an issue about the quality of some teleworking jobs[6], for example working for a single employee providing a telephone service may be relatively low paid compared to teleworking in professional or technical occupations. It is important, however, to consider what the alternative would be; where this is commuting to an urban location everyday or not working then teleworking will provide major benefits for rural areas. Teleworking can also lead to significant reduction in congestion at peak times, for example, a 1996 US study found that for those moving to teleworking, vehicle miles fell by 63%. Overall, given the benefits, there is a good case for considering ways to facilitate teleworking.

e) *Rural post offices*

10.30 Post offices play a key role in the commercial and community life of many rural areas. As well as public services, such as payment of social security benefits, over four fifths of rural post offices are also the village shop. Despite an average of about 200 closures a year, the Post Office estimates that 80-85% of the rural population lives within 1 mile of a post office and the vast majority of people are within a few miles.

10.31 The Post Office White Paper[7] sets out the Government's plans for the future of the Post Office. A key element of these plans is the automation of Post Office counters. This could allow post offices to become agents for banks and to serve as a platform for the electronic delivery of Government services, including the electronic payment of benefits. As a consequence, the Post Office should be well placed to bid for any business under the proposal that low-cost ICT access centres should be set up in rural areas. This should be reflected within the business strategy that is being developed by the Post Office.

10.32 The White Paper commits the Government to develop access criteria for post offices, to ensure the retention of an appropriate post office network across the country – including rural areas. The work on access criteria will need to tackle the question of which services are most important and the best means of facilitating their provision.

The role of market towns

10.33 The term 'market towns' is used broadly in this report: it includes all settlements that serve as a focus for services and economic activity for rural hinterlands. Market towns have a crucial role to play within rural economies. By co-locating employment, services and housing they can act as key centres for the delivery of public and private services to their surrounding rural areas and as centres for employment opportunities. Market towns can provide a sufficiently large market to enable businesses and other service providers to benefit from scale economies and achieve a critical mass to provide a viable range of services. There are also transport benefits from concentrating services and economic activities together, particularly where they can be served by public transport.

10.34 But market towns have been under pressure from:

- economic restructuring;

- a loss of traditional activities such as livestock markets;

- the shift of services to larger towns; and

- the growth in out-of-town retailing.

10.35 It is important for rural communities that market towns retain their vitality. In many cases, initiatives have helped to do this (see Box 10C).

[6] RDC (1996), *'Teleworking and rural development'*, rural research report No 27.
[7] CM4340, 8 July 1999.

Box 10C: Revitalising market towns

Bishop's Castle, Shropshire has a population of 1,570 and serves a surrounding community of 9,000. Following the closure of the town's two largest employers with the loss of 150 jobs, the local District Council, in partnership with other parts of local government, the voluntary sector and the private sector, secured £6.3m funding including £1m Rural Challenge funding. A not-for-profit company limited by guarantee was set up with the task of regenerating the area and diversifying the economy away from agriculture.

The company involved the local community as early as possible, through community workshops and focus groups, to ensure that they had ownership and support of the project. The company have since converted redundant premises to provide 37 small business units; established an IT resource centre; provided 200 child care places to allow women to return to work; given grants/loans to allow 60 local businesses to get business efficiency advice; supported 52 tourist projects; given grants to support small arts, transport, and social projects; and improved drainage to allow social housing to be built.

As a result of the scheme 168 jobs were created or preserved; 156 people in the area secured employment; 450 businesses received advice; and 1,400 people directly benefited from the new facilities. Rural Challenge funding also led the local district council to give higher priority to the building of 6 new village halls and the refurbishment of others.

Bakewell, Derbyshire has a population of 4,000 and serves a surrounding community of 22,000. Tourism is of growing importance to the area; the agricultural economy was focussed on an ageing and dilapidated town centre livestock market that, without action, was likely to have to close by the year 2000; and traffic congestion in the town centre was becoming a major problem. The Bakewell Project centred on the relocation of the livestock market, the construction of an Agricultural and Business Centre and the regeneration of the town centre. The total cost of the project was £17 million, of which just over half was private sector funding. Public funding came from Rural Challenge, SRB, the district council, TEC, Business Links and European Objective 5b funds.

There was some local opposition to the project, including concerns that new market centre would be on a greenfield site and would affect the character of the town. Public opinion has been won over by getting the local community involved through quarterly meetings, a regular newsletter and a drop-in information centre. The community has also helped shape the project. For example, the community centre was built entirely by local labour. And local schoolchildren and volunteers were closely involved in a biodiversity project that formed part of the development, providing new habitats in and around the access bridge for bats, otters and voles, as well as establishing new wildflowers, trees and plants.

The Agriculture and Business Centre includes conference, exhibition and training facilities, the local business link, a café, retail units and parking for tourist coaches. Regeneration of the town centre included building a supermarket; shops and business premises; a swimming pool; a modern library; a community centre; and a mixed housing development. An independent study found that by the year 2001 the project should generate £35m income for the local economy, protect over 500 local jobs and create up to 370 new jobs.

10.36 Enhancing the economic dynamism of rural areas will greatly assist market towns and so will modernising agriculture. Spreading best practice and mobilising local initiatives will be one of the most important measures: for example, building upon the work of 'Action for Market Towns' – a national organisation to assist market towns supported by the Countryside Agency. But there is scope for Government to do more. In effect, Government should consider confirming the role of market towns as key economic and social centres in rural areas. In particular there is a case for government making a 'New Commitment' to Market Towns, which would recognise the critical role they play in economic and social life as well as the maintenance of rural economies, and bolster their position. This commitment can be realised in part by more effective integration of the wide-ranging existing initiatives, for example:-

- rural business grants, support for the rural bus network, ICT-based initiatives, installation of IT in libraries.

- the role of RDAs in designing rural development programmes targeted on their most deprived areas, administrating the single regeneration budget and other regeneration activities, and applying for additional EU funding. Their regional economic strategies should also explicitly recognise and foster the role of market towns.

- the use of planning policy to encourage new retail development in or on the edge of town centres (rather than out-of-town). This is supported by the Government's 'town centre first' approach to planning for supermarkets. Large retail suppliers should also be encouraged to adopt strategies to support small stores and local produce.

- a range of regeneration initiatives, some of which could be part-funded from EU budgets;

- a strategy to bolster rural service provision by concentrating resources on outlets based in market towns;

- the use of the planning system to sustain and enhance the viability of market towns as key retail centres; and

10.37 The commitment could also be supplemented with new initiatives. One example would be the establishment of Business Improvement Districts.

10.38 The vitality of market towns and their ability to provide a range of services to their rural hinterland depends on the presence of an attractive retail business centre. For retail businesses, commercial wealth is linked to the quality of the public environment. If this does not attract people – visitors, residents and those from the surrounding area – sales will fall and profits will vanish. It is in the collective interest of shops, service businesses, banks, cafes and restaurants therefore to invest in their local centres.

10.39 Mechanisms to deliver such investment have been hard to establish. In the United States, some town-centre property owners and retailers have come together to create Business Improvement Districts. For a set period (renewable by a business vote), the property owners/retailers agree to pay a supplementary rate. This income flow can then be used to lever in finance for the investments such as pedestrian infrastructure improvement and improving amenities within the town centre. Once united in a Business Improvement District, the retailers often find it easier to collaborate on schemes that deliver a collective benefit, such as late night opening and joint promotions.

10.40 The application of this idea in the United Kingdom has been frustrated by a combination of fears of free-riding (retailers who fail to join a voluntary scheme may still benefit, so why should anyone join?) and public finance constraints (a compulsory levy could be classified as a new tax). The Urban Task Force argues that something more than the voluntary schemes operated a few larger towns is needed. They suggest that if a certain percentage of businesses want a Town Improvement Zone, then everyone should be required to contribute. Their model envisages contributions from central and local government – reflecting the public service benefit of vital and viable town centres – and a new statutory basis.

10.41 These arguments are of particular importance in market towns which require improvements in public facilities. This is closely related to the proposal in the Local Government White Paper.[8] The Government intends to consult on the details of a scheme to allow councils to set a supplementary local rate of up to 5% of the national rate, or to give a rebate. This would help finance additional discretionary spending on priorities agreed with the local business community. The Government might also allow beacon councils greater freedom to set local business rates, up to a further 5% maximum. In this case, councils may be able to levy the additional local rate across the whole of their area, just part of it, or on specific classes of business ratepayer, providing that councils secure the agreement of the affected ratepayers. In some cases, this would provide a mechanism for implementing Business Improvement Districts or Town Improvement Zones.

10.42 The DETR has already put a number of proposals forward for consideration, and within this they should examine the feasibility of establishing Town Improvement Zones for country towns, where the majority of retailers and other service businesses agree. It would be important to consider whether the existing business rates proposals provide sufficient flexibility, or whether further flexibility in line with the Urban Task Force's recommendation is needed.

10.43 The available evidence supports the view that small businesses occupy properties with lower rateable values – predominantly those up to £5,000. The Government is also considering the introduction of measures to reduce the rating burden on small businesses. This would be useful for small rural businesses in villages and market towns (to the extent that these businesses have rateable values below £5,000), for which business rates can be a major burden.

10.44 In summary, there is merit in considering the integration of existing and new initiatives of relevance to market towns. One way to do this would be to pilot a 'New Commitment to Market Towns', where all these initiatives would be drawn together at a limited number of locations before a more extensive roll-out. RDAs would have a key role in the selection of these pilot towns – and, in implementing the New Commitment, would work in partnership with local authorities, business representatives and others.

Rural transport

10.45 Rural transport represents the lifeblood of rural communities. It has a vital role to play in providing access to work and to services. Rural transport needs to be considered against the backdrop of the Integrated Transport White Paper,[9] which is putting in place a range of policies to improve public transport including the new statutory rail authority, bus quality partnerships, Local Transport Plans (LTPs) and tools for local authorities to combat congestion. These policies are intended to tackle growing congestion and pollution from car use not be restricting access to the car, but by reducing the need to use cars for such a high proportion of journeys by providing reliable and high-quality alternatives through investment in public transport.

8   *Modern Local Government: in Touch with the People*, DETR 1998.

9   *A new deal for transport: Better for everyone*, July 1998, CM 3950.

10.46 At present, in town and country alike, around a third of adults do not have access to a car. For them, a transport policy which relied on the car would be disastrous. But so would attempts to force people to give up a car on which they have come to rely. That is why car usage, rather than car ownership, is the key issue in considering the balance between public and private transport.

10.47 Improving access to transport for rural dwellers is a challenge, to which there are four main strands:

- recognising the key role of private transport – for many people who live and work in rural communities, access to a car is the only practicable means of undertaking many journeys;

- better marketing, quality and stability of bus services – rural bus services are important as a means of linking rural dwellers to key service access centres, such as market towns;

- more flexibility for community transport services – to meet gaps in services that cannot be met cost-effectively by public transport requires more flexible services, responsive to individuals' needs; and

- much stronger and proactive integration and co-ordination of all the different transport services (e.g. bus services, voluntary minibuses, school buses, ambulances and hospital minibuses etc.)

10.48 Much of this is already taking place as a result of the White Paper. This section considers areas where further progress could help.

a) *Private transport*

10.49 The car is the most important means of transport for most rural journeys. The large range of different urban and rural destinations of rural travellers means that any one journey is too thinly trafficked for conventional public transport to be feasible.

There is a tension, therefore, between the objective of improving accessibility, which the Government recognises for many rural journeys requires car transport, and measures to reduce car use in places where it is creating environmental damage through congestion or air pollution. Over time there is more scope to influence travel patterns through location decisions, planning policy and step changes in the quality of public transport. But cars will continue to play the key role for many rural journeys.

10.50 The necessity of the car for many rural journeys is indicated by the much higher proportion of low-income households in rural areas who own a car compared to the national average. The rise in the costs of fuel has been a particular concern, though the rise in motoring costs is less significant than is often supposed: Family Expenditure Survey data shows motoring costs remaining relatively constant as a proportion of average household expenditure over the last 5 years. But costs are still a significant constraint for the poorest rural households needing to run cars, who are disproportionately affected by any increase in fuel costs.

10.51 Helping low-income rural households whose mobility will be reduced by increases in fuel costs might be done through targeted assistance for certain groups. For example, there are New Deal schemes offering short-term bicycle loans, moped loans, payment of fares on public transport, driving lesson subsidies and grants for the repair and maintenance of motor vehicles (see Box 10D). The Government could encourage the extension of these schemes to other rural areas, possibly using vouchers to cover public transport and taxi fares and motoring costs. This proposal has links with the concessionary fares schemes already operated by many local authorities, which is to be reviewed by the Commission for Integrated Transport (CfIT) in the light of the Government's commitment to

Box 10D: The New Deal and Transport Schemes

Cornwall – the Employment Service and the RDC co-operated to provide information and a map on buses, trains, community car schemes and taxis, and introduced a rural transport subsidy scheme which paid new deal clients' fares for 6-8 weeks. Clients were expected to save their wages in order to tax or MOT vehicles that they would have otherwise been unable to use. The cost of the scheme was £10,000 met by the RDC and Kerrier district council.

North Herefordshire and South Shropshire – the RDC, local councils and TECs have funded the Wheels 2 Work scheme since 1995. This helps 16-25 year old new deal clients with a job or training opportunity. Clients can lease a moped on a six month contract; apply for vehicle repair and maintenance grants of £80 to £300 to cover road tax, MOT, minor repairs, new tyres; and apply for subsidised driving lessons and cost of one test (average cost of the subsidy is £240 per person).

a minimum standard for concessionary bus fares for older people.

10.52 Where road user charging is introduced in towns or cities it is important that this takes account of the implications for surrounding rural areas. The policy that some of the revenue from road user charging and car parking levies, indicated in the White Paper daughter document,[10] should be used to fund transport improvements outside the area is a useful step. The Government needs to ensure that revenues raised are, in part, used to improve access to urban centres for people who live in rural communities – for example, through low cost park and ride schemes. The interdependence of town and countryside is evident here.

10.53 A large number of informal car lifts are provided in rural areas, but there is scope to encourage much more systematic car sharing by rural dwellers (e.g. sharing cars for trips to work, possibly as part of a green commuting plan). Another possibility is car clubs, where a number of cars are jointly owned or leased by a group of households. Cars are booked out when needed, with a fixed fee for entry and a charge for use. Car clubs are well established in Germany and Switzerland and are being piloted in Edinburgh and Leeds. A village car pool scheme could be a useful

way of improving rural accessibility, while reducing the household costs and the transport impacts of households owning a car. The private sector would be able to run car clubs, though demonstration projects to test the concept and stimulate the market would be needed. ICT would play an important role in administering a car club and it would also be a way of co-ordinating and encouraging car sharing.

b) *Rural public and commercial transport*

10.54 Public transport has a key role to play in facilitating access for rural dwellers, both as a substitute to using the car and for those who do not have access to private transport, especially to key rural economic centres such as market towns. Funding for rural public transport in England was given a boost of £41.7m in the 1998 budget and this has been increased by an extra £10m for the following two years. DETR estimate that this has led to 18,000 new or enhanced services. Before any decision on future levels of support for rural transport are taken, it will be necessary to review the impact on service levels and patronage of the new funding.

10.55 Improvements to public transport in rural areas raise a number of challenges. The first is to determine the most appropriate

[10] DETR (1998), *Breaking the Logjam.*

network of bus services. Rural networks need to provide good access to the market towns or large villages – which are acting as the main centres for service delivery – as well as reflecting local needs and circumstances. Transport needs could be assessed by Parish councils and within village appraisals (discussed in Chapter 8) as one way of developing the local input into the development of local transport plans and rural bus quality partnerships. These will also need to take account of local strategies for delivering services.

10.56 The second challenge is to ensure greater stability in the funding of public transport. This is important because it can take time for knowledge of local bus services to be acquired (especially by car drivers); and there needs to be a confidence in the reliability and stability of bus services before people will switch to it. (One commercial operator uses the rule of thumb that bus patronage takes around three years to build up). Significant fluctuations or drops in services will increase uncertainty and encourage people to stick with or switch to their cars.

10.57 The third challenge is to develop the integration of different modes of transport, particularly through the role of Local Authorities. There are significant transport benefits and costs savings from joining up

Box 10E: Devon County Council – A Co-ordinated approach to the planning and provision of Rural Transport

Devon County Council has developed an integrated approach to the planning, management and provision of organised passenger transport services through its Transport Co-ordination Service (TCS). The unit covers school transport, social services transport, public, rural and community transport and the in-house fleet and also extends into the wider public sector. It aims to provide the high quality transport services through the most effective use of resources.

The approach of the TCS has raised standards, produced savings and promoted innovation on a wide scale. Partnerships have been created with a range of organisations including bus and rail operators, statutory agencies, national and local charities, community groups, parish councils, district councils and health authorities. The result has been to provide local and integrated bus services as well as school transport, concessionary fares and public transport access to the countryside. There has also been tailor made transport for schools and social services, community buses, ring and ride schemes, community car schemes, shopmobility and public transport information and promotion.

The increasing importance of individual provision of services has been recognised and the process has identified gaps in provision and transport needs are not being satisfactory met. To address this, the TCS has been developing Local Transport Partnerships, linking with Devon social services and health authorities.

The local transport partnerships programme is being co-ordinated under the Devon Rural Transport Partnership, funded by the Government's new Rural Transport Partnership scheme. It is intended to have countywide coverage by next year of 15 local partnerships based on market towns and adjoining parishes, all linked by a computer network. These will have an important role in identifying local needs and gaps in services whilst also operating new services.

different transport services. For example, separate mini-buses are operated by Community transport schemes, schools, health authorities along with school buses and contract services. Devon County Council's Transport Co-ordination Service is one good model (of many) for linking together different transport networks (see Box 10E). The Rural Transport Partnership (RTP) already provides one effective tool for co-ordination, though it would be desirable for RTP schemes to be closely tied in with the integration of services within local transport plans.

10.58 There need to be improvements in the marketing of public transport. Better marketing and information of rural bus services is vital. The recently published daughter document on bus services[11] suggests a range of measures to improve bus services, including bus priority schemes and bus quality partnerships. Bus quality partnerships will provide higher quality services, better information and better marketing of bus services. Developing a rural bus quality partnerships should be a high priority. The use of ICT will also be a way of providing better information on, and marketing of, bus services.

c) *Voluntary and community transport*

10.59 Voluntary transport is important in rural areas where public transport alone cannot cater for the wide variety of journeys made by the dispersed population. Voluntary and community transport schemes have become increasingly important in rural areas, growing from a few hundred a decade ago to over 5,000 today. Box 10F overleaf sets out a range of services that are being successfully provided in Derbyshire through community transport. The main problems encountered by voluntary transport schemes have been the high costs; lack of information which might generate demand; difficulty in

attracting and maintaining volunteers; regulatory constraints and uncertain funding. There are a number of steps that could be taken to improve voluntary transport e.g. reducing regulatory constraints and simplifying bureaucracy tied to funding.

10.60 Voluntary transport providers regard the legal constraints on voluntary and community transport sector (resulting from the 1985 Transport Act) as significant. Discussions with the voluntary transport sector suggest that reducing these constraints would remove significant barriers upon the voluntary sector. Key problems include:

- Community buses running a local bus service operate under Section 22 of the 1985 Act, with timetables and routes registered with the Traffic Commissioner. These registered bus services cannot use paid drivers, so when there are staff shortages they can not attract additional staff by offering payments, nor can a paid scheme manager fill in if drivers are absent.

- Door-to-door community transport schemes operate under Section 19 of the 1985 Act, which allows the provision of services to specific groups, such as the mobility impaired or those accessing health services. But the Act prevents voluntary transport schemes from offering services to the wider travelling public, which would help integrate services and create extra revenue.

10.61 One way of easing the constraints on the voluntary and community sector, as suggested in a report for DETR on voluntary transport,[12] would be to introduce a new community transport permit. If this could be done solely by placing more stringent conditions on door-to-door schemes, then it might be better to amend existing sections of legislation. The main drawback to any

---

[11] DETR (1999), *From Workhorse to Thoroughbred: A Better Role for Bus Travel.*
[12] Steer, Davies and Gleave, DETR (1999), *Review of Voluntary Transport.*

Box 10F: Derbyshire Community Transport

Community transport forms an important part of the public transport system in Derbyshire. Between them, the eight local schemes cover the whole of the county, providing a comprehensive service. The schemes provide a number of pre-bookable services, including:

- **Dial-a-bus** – a "door-to-town" transport service, supplementing public transport for those who experience difficulties with conventional transport;

- **Dial-a-ride** – a flexible "door-to-door" service for those who experience difficulties with conventional transport;

- **Group hire** – transport for groups involved in community activities (e.g. scouts, schools, luncheon clubs and church groups);

- **Social car scheme** – similar to dial-a-ride but provided by volunteers in their own cars (they receive a mileage allowance on a non-profit basis);

- **Shopmobility** – providing electric wheelchairs and scooters to access shops and other facilities within the town centre (typically integrated with the dial-a-bus service to the town centre);

- **Community Bus** – a scheduled service similar to a normal bus route, regular passengers who cannot get to a bus stop can pre-book seats and the bus will make a small diversion to pick them up, the service can also pick up members of the public along the route.

In a typical month, the dial-a-bus, dial-a-ride and group hire services will cover over 65,000 miles, providing 76,000 passenger journeys. Each of the eight local schemes operates as a registered charity.

Running costs are recovered via group hire charges, dial-a-ride fares, dial-a-bus fares and subsidies, and contracts for services to the county council (e.g. education and social services). The schemes also rely heavily on volunteer drivers, actively fund-raise from the public and, occasionally, they benefit from one-off grants from the Rural Transport Development Fund, Help the Aged, the National Lotteries Charities Board, and Opportunities for Volunteering (Department of Health funding). In addition, Derbyshire County Council provides direct support – in the form of grants and the support from their Public Transport Unit.

changes is that commercial operators might complain about unfair competition, as community schemes can in some circumstances operate under less stringent requirements. In theory, voluntary services should not be operating where a commercial service would be effective; and if voluntary organisations bid for contract work they must meet the same conditions as commercial operators. But an expanded role for community transport in conveying some paying passengers, may divert some demand from commercial services.

10.62 The need for greater flexibility and integration between services to meet rural needs, does, however, point to allowing paid drivers to operate community bus services and for removing restrictions on whom can be carried under door-to door voluntary transport schemes. If the less stringent conditions for voluntary transport give them a significant competitive advantage then it may be better to consider whether the commercial operators on these routes can also be given more flexibility.

10.63 More generally, to get an effective and integrated rural service, the barriers between the voluntary and the commercial services need to be broken down and the sectors should be encouraged to work together in partnership, given the potential synergies between their operations. It would also be desirable to explore relaxing restrictions on the use of other transport services used by public bodies, such as school buses.

10.64 The Government funds allocated via the Rural Transport Partnership have led to the employment of 38 community transport officers, who provide an audit of all voluntary services and look for gaps and synergies between services. It would be useful for all counties either to have community transport officers or an alternative co-ordinating mechanism. These officers could take the lead in: joining up services; making the links with commercial operators; and assisting rural communities in appraising transport needs. Local Transport Plan guidance highlights the benefits to authorities of integration of voluntary transport within the overall processes of planning and provision, but not all local authorities have included community transport representatives within the process.

10.65 The bureaucracy tied to funding applications, and the suggestion that funding streams should be more closely aligned is discussed earlier. Providing funding for community transport schemes for three years ahead would remove another major administrative burden and greatly assist improvements in service provision by allowing planning to be based on more certainty about funding.

10.66 Fuel duty rebate is available for registered bus and community service schemes (section 22), but not door to door schemes (under section 19). In principle, there is a case for equal treatment of registered services and more flexible door-to-door services, though this should depend upon an assessment of the costs, benefit and practicalities. This will be considered by the CfIT review of public subsidies for buses. The CfIT review should also consider the proposals in the 1998 budget for using the Fuel Duty Rebate to assist rural buses and greener buses. Switching the rebate to a mileage basis from a fuel consumption basis would encourage greater use of small and mini buses operating in rural areas, and should also be addressed.

Housing

10.67 Housing is a major issue facing local rural areas and is of considerable importance to the viability of rural economies and rural communities. In broad terms, there are two main challenges facing policy-makers. The first concerns the predicted amount of additional housing required in rural areas over the coming decades. The second is the present and continuing need for more affordable housing in rural areas. The Countryside Agency's 1999 survey of rural trends[13] estimates that the number of households in rural districts is projected to increase by 1m from 1991 to 2011. And the report notes that there was an estimated need for 80,000 additional affordable homes in rural areas between 1990 and 1995; but, since 1990, less than 18,000 have been built.

10.68 Housing relates closely to each of the objectives for rural economies outlined in Chapter 6. First, in facilitating economic dynamism, there is a link between demographic changes and economic

---

[13] Countryside Agency (1999), *The State of the Countryside.*

development opportunities in rural areas, as well as important links between the operation of local housing and labour markets. Second, in ensuring that development is environmentally sustainable, there is a need for careful consideration of the use of greenfield and brownfield sites, and the implications of new development for traffic generation, the rural landscape and biodiversity. Third, in ensuring more equitable access to economic and social opportunities in rural areas, the provision of affordable housing and its role in the maintenance or promotion of 'balanced rural communities' will be of pressing importance.

10.69 Unfortunately, as was observed in a recent report by the Rural Development Commission, 'the provision of affordable housing in rural areas is caught in a spiral'.[14] Concerns about household growth are leading to tighter planning controls and restrictions – which, in turn, are driving up the cost of new-build housing to levels that make it increasingly difficult for Registered Social Landlords to expand the supply of social housing in rural areas while meeting financial targets set by the Housing Corporation. And, particularly in the South-East, private-rented and owner-occupier sectors of the housing market are becoming more expensive as trends of in-migration from urban areas continue to create demand for rural housing – so that in some rural areas, housing becomes accessible only to the very rich or the (housing benefit-assisted) very poor.

10.70 The Government has already taken steps to increase investment in housing. Over the life of the current Parliament an additional £5bn is being made available for housing investment in rural and urban areas. Some of this money is being directed through local authorities, which are well placed to assess local needs and priorities.

Other resources are allocated to the Housing Corporation's Rural Programme, to support new social housing in rural areas. But there may be scope to do more. The PIU project has identified a number of areas that could usefully be explored as part of the research for the Rural White Paper:

- the extent to which planning guidance needs to be amended to allow local authorities to differentiate in development plans between social, affordable and private housing;

- whether development plans should specifically select areas which are only for social and affordable housing;

- the advantages of concentrating affordable and social housing in small market towns or other locations where a comprehensive range of services and job opportunities are available, including the benefits of development on brown field sites which help to prevent new greenfield development and hence protect the countryside;

- the need for any new housing developments to take account of access to services, and transport requirements, including public transport links and if necessary facilitate the provision of such services as a condition of development; and

- whether there needs to be additional support for Registered Social Landlords to increase the supply of social housing in rural communities.

- whether Registered Social Landlords operating in rural areas should be given more flexibility to include non-housing elements such as a shop, pub, offices or workshops in their developments, to provide additional services or employment in rural areas.

[14] Rural Development Commission (1998), *A Home in the Country? Affordable Housing Needs in Rural England.*

Machinery of Government

10.71 There is a need to consider whether the existing structures and mechanisms of government are appropriate and sufficient to deliver the policy objectives set out in this report. Three issues can usefully be considered at this stage: the organisation of government at regional level; the mechanisms for policy co-ordination and evaluation; and the role of the Countryside Agency.

a) *Regional organisation*

10.72 The regional organisation of MAFF, DETR and other Departments is likely to be a key factor in the effective delivery of the objectives. The key organisations are:

- MAFF's Regional Service Centres (RSCs) – the majority of work is processing claims for CAP payments. The RSCs also undertake some policy-related functions on Structural Funds and agri-environment schemes, and represent MAFF HQ within the regions.

- Farming and Rural Conservation Agency (FRCA), an Executive Agency of MAFF which provides policy advice and technical support to Government on a wide range of issues, including agri-environment and rural economy schemes, land use planning and rural development, environmental protection, wildlife management and milk hygiene.

- Government Offices in the Regions (GOs), which currently comprise DETR, DfEE, DCMS, Home Office and DTI and cover a range of functions, including planning, transport, housing, Structural Funds and business advice, innovation and competitiveness, training and environment protection.

- Regional Development Agencies (RDAs), which are Non-Departmental Public Bodies and came into being this year to take forward regional economic strategies, regeneration and Structural Funds. In developing regional economic strategies, RDAs have a specific remit to consider the rural dimension.

10.73 A number of developments – the implementation of the Rural Development Regulation, the greater emphasis on the links between agriculture and the environment, the importance of economic diversification for agriculture, the advent of the RDAs, and the PIU study of the Role of Central Government at Regional and Local Levels – highlight the need to consider closer integration between MAFF's regional organisations and the GOs. The existing concordats between GOs and MAFF's RSCs and FRCA are being strengthened to facilitate closer co-operation and better co-ordination of policies. But this may well not provide the level of integration which is desirable for the longer term.

10.74 The project research supports the argument for restructuring at the regional level. Other than the need to maintain an efficient CAP payment system, the main practical challenges for MAFF's regional organisation over the next few years will be to deliver the final stages of the Objective 5b funding programme and, more importantly, to develop the arrangements for administering the new Structural Funds and the Rural Development Regulation. The general principle here should be that MAFF and GOs have the authority to deliver these programmes as effectively as possible. From the MAFF perspective this might involve increasing regional discretion. For example, where schemes have multiple funders, the different funding partners should be able to process applications to broadly the same timetable, and ideally the decision making should be integrated.

10.75 On this basis, there is a strong case for, over time, moving the policy related aspects of the Structural Funds and Rural Development Regulation activities in MAFF's Regional Service Centres into the Government Offices. This is likely to entail bringing elements of the work currently carried out by the Farming and Rural Conservation Agency (FRCA) in the Regions within the remit of the GOs. The presumption is that the staff within the Government Offices would be able to represent all of MAFF's policy areas, within the region. This is likely to prove the most effective way of ensuring greater integration of planning matters, the implementation of the Rural Development Regulation, and greater integration of agriculture with mainstream economic strategies and environmental policies. It could also help link together other services such as one-stop shops for business advice to farmers and funding. This would be consistent with the emerging conclusions of the PIU study on the Role Central Government at the Regional and Local Level.

10.76 GOs ought to work closely with the RDAs in taking forward rural policies and strategies. MAFF staff within GOs would have four important roles in this respect. First, ensuring that the development of policy on the Rural Development Regulation and Structural Funds takes account of the regional economic strategies. Second, making sure that when regional planning guidance and the RDA's regional economic strategies are being developed, full account is taken of MAFF's policy issues and the role of food production, processing and distribution in regional economies. Third, ensuring that better links are made between MAFF policies and policies of other Government departments and of local authorities (for example in relation to social exclusion) where GOs are well placed to make such links: establishing such links is an area of growing

importance, which is also being highlighted in the PIU study on the Role of Central Government at the Regional and Local Level. Fourth, providing a strong regional dimension to national policy-making.

10.77 MAFF is reviewing the future organisation of the CAP payment function of its Regional Service Centres with a view to improving efficiency and customer service delivery as a major new IT system becomes operational over the next two to three years. The review is scheduled to be completed by the end of 1999. In parallel with that review, MAFF should consider developing a detailed plan for integrating its work on the development of rural policies and strategies at regional level with the GOs. This plan should address the future organisation of all the non-CAP scheme processing functions of the RSCs and the the FRCA's activities at regional level on rural economy and development, land use planning, wildlife management and agri-environment schemes. Decisions will need to be taken on whether the FRCA should remain as an Executive Agency providing services to the GOs on a similar basis as to MAFF and other customers, or whether its functions and staff should be absorbed into GOs, MAFF HQ, MAFF and RSCs as appropriate.

b) *Policy development, co-ordination and review*

10.78 The agenda for reform set out in this report would require the efforts of a number of government departments and agencies, as well as other stakeholder groups. Arrangements for taking forward policy development could include:

- designation of a lead Minister (possibly the Minister designated to chair the Cabinet Committee on rural affairs) to oversee progress and ensure effective integration of future work arising from this report with the work to produce, and then take forward, the Rural White Paper;

- reflection of the new objectives for rural economies in the forthcoming countryside Public Service Agreement (PSA), to be prepared jointly by MAFF and DETR;

- consideration of the financial issues raised in the report in forthcoming decisions on taxation and expenditure policy (including the next Spending Review).

10.79 Looking more widely, there is also a range of institutional options (set out in Box 10G overleaf) for improving the development, co-ordination and review of policy for rural areas. In addition to these options, the Government has recently established a Cabinet Committee on rural affairs.

c) *The role of the Countryside Agency*

10.80 The new Countryside Agency – established in April 1999 – clearly has a key role to play in delivering the objectives for rural economies. It is well placed to maintain a close relationship with Ministers and the policy-making process while, at the same time, operating at an arm's length. There are four key functions for the Countryside Agency to fulfil in the further development of policies for rural areas. These are to:

- undertake research and development activities to help inform policy-making;

- pilot innovative schemes in rural areas;

- monitor the performance of rural areas and publishing an annual report on the state of the countryside (including a commentary on the progress and effectiveness of Government policy); and

- undertake what can be termed 'rural-proofing'.

10.81 'Rural-proofing' is the process whereby all Government policy is evaluated to a test to determine the impact it will have on rural areas. Essentially, it would involve Government departments formally consulting the body charged with rural-proofing at an

appropriate stage in the development of policy to consider whether a proposed policy has any implications for rural areas – and, if it does, whether these implications are sufficient to warrant modification of the policy of some other adjustment (for example, a change in funding or in service delivery mechanisms). Rural-proofing would allow the Government to build in to policy-making a thorough consideration of all needs of rural areas – not just those needs addressed by the work of MAFF and DETR but also those addressed by policies on local government, housing, education and employment, health and social services, trade and industry, home affairs and culture. Of course, it is possible to envisage changes to the organisation of central government that would require the need for a designated rural-proofer. But if rural-proofing were required, the Countryside Agency would be a strong candidate for the task.

10.82 Aside from the issue of rural-proofing, the Countryside Agency could play a significant part in taking forward the conclusions of this report. It could be charged with further development of some of the suggested pilot schemes (e.g. in relation to service delivery and transport); it could assist with research and information – gathering (e.g. in relation to economic, environmental and social issues); and it could monitor performance on key issues (e.g. the provision of business advice in rural areas).

d) *Better information for rural policy making*

10.83 The development of policy on rural issues would be made easier by tackling the lack of consistent and comprehensive data on rural economies. Particular problems include:

- the lack of a consistent definition of rural areas – the PIU project uncovered a wide range of different definitions within Government alone;

Box 10G: Potential options for Improved Policy Development, co-ordination and review

(a) **External 'enforcer'** – a lead minister in the Cabinet Office to champion rural issues. The latter has the disadvantage of placing political responsibility for rural issues at an institutional distance from the day-to-day work.

(b) **Network of Ministers** – on similar lines to the 'social exclusion' or 'green' ministers would help to improve the profile and cross-departmental communication of rural issues, though too many networks might reduce the effectiveness of each.

(c) **Central rural unit** – along the lines of the Women's Unit or the Social Exclusion Unit. Such a unit could help raise the profile of rural issues across Whitehall. But to be effective, it would require direct ministerial support – probably from the Prime Minister or a Minister with Cabinet Office responsibilities; and there are severe limits to the number of units for which this support could be made available.

(d) **Sounding Board/'Rural Round Table' for England** – to bring together a range of people and organisations with an interest in rural issues, to help inform government policy-making. The purpose of the Round Table would be to assemble the principal stakeholders in rural England – commercial interests (including those from the agriculture sector), voluntary organisations (including the major environmental and community groups) and elected representatives – to discuss issues of concern to the Government and rural people. It would provide the Government with an opportunity to float policy options and consult on policy proposals at an early stage. By adopting this broader remit the Round Table could differentiate itself effectively from the work of the Countryside Agency Board (which would continue to concentrate on the narrower task of overseeing the work of the Agency).

(e) **The Executive could suggest to Parliament that it might wish to create Parliamentary Select Committees on rural issues.** This would create authoritative new bodies to scrutinise the development and delivery of rural policy. Their establishment would require changes to the remit of existing select committees (particularly those covering Agriculture and Environment), in order to avoid duplication. Disadvantages would be that a 'rural' committee could marginalise the issues, taking them away from consideration in Department-related committees. Conversely, many policies affecting rural areas (such as on planning or the environment) would still remain with other committees. Nevertheless, a new committee working alongside others could have a useful role in providing a holistic overview of rural issues and identifying the policy overlaps, and might be necessary if the option of a pooled budget is pursued. An alternative would be for one of the existing committees formally to expand its remit to take on rural affairs.

- the difficulty in analysing social exclusion in rural areas given the dispersed nature of rural poverty, which makes average incomes of limited value, but given small sample sizes it is difficult to take disaggregation too far;

- the difficulty of identifying overall levels of public expenditure in rural areas; and

- limited analysis of the rural dimension in economic data and limited coverage of financial statistics on agriculture.

10.84 These information deficiencies will be a continual constraint on addressing rural issues and rural policy. A number of ways to improve the quality of the data have been identified. First, researchers and statisticians from the Countryside Agency, Office of National Statistics (ONS), DETR and MAFF should consider setting up a task force to agree a small set of rural definitions, which they will adopt for themselves and promulgate their use in official statistics and to other organisations. Second, to address social exclusion within rural areas is likely to need a bottom-up approach based upon survey information, rather than being easily picked up within national statistics. Third, it would also be useful for ONS and others to provide a spatial breakdown of data on an annual basis between rural and other areas. Fourth, the economic data could be revised to provide: a breakdown of the 'services' data category, separating out tourism, recreation, and the other components of the service sector of the economy; better information on ICT; more comprehensive information on total incomes of farm households; and financial statistics for agriculture, including rates of return on capital.

ANNEX A1. THE WORK OF THE PERFORMANCE AND INNOVATION UNIT

The creation of the Performance and Innovation Unit (PIU) was announced by the Prime Minister on 28 July 1998 as part of the changes following a review of the effectiveness of the centre of Government by Sir Richard Wilson. The PIU's aim is to improve the capacity of Government to address strategic, cross-cutting issues and promote innovation in the development of policy and in the delivery of the Government's objectives. The PIU is part of the drive for better, more joined-up government. It acts as a resource for the whole of government, tackling issues that cross public sector institutional boundaries on a project basis.

The Unit reports direct to the Prime Minister through Sir Richard Wilson and is headed by a Senior Civil Servant, Mr Suma Chakrabarti. It has a small central team that helps recommend project subjects, manages the Unit's work and follows up projects' recommendations with departments. Work on the projects themselves is carried out by small teams assembled both from inside and outside government. About half of the current project team staff are drawn from outside Whitehall, including from private sector consultancies, academia and local government.

The first set of PIU projects was announced by the Prime Minister in December 1998. The aim is to complete most of them by the end of 1999.

The projects are:

- **Developing Electronic Commerce in the UK** – how to make the UK the world's best environment for electronic commerce, ensuring that the UK benefits fully from the single fastest growing marketplace in the global economy;

- **Active Ageing** – how to improve the well-being and quality of life of older people by helping them to remain active. The study will identify ways of increasing the employment opportunities for older people, by examining the incentives for businesses to employ and retain older people and for individuals to remain in paid or voluntary work;

- **Central Government's Role at Regional & Local Level** – getting the right institutional arrangements and relationships in place for joined-up delivery of central Government policies in regions and communities;

- **Accountability and Incentives for Joined-Up Government** – examining how current accountability arrangements and incentive systems can be reformed to facilitate joined-up policy-making and delivery, for example by promoting achievement of joint objectives which require co-operation between departments; and

- **Objectives for Rural Economies** – examining the differing needs of local rural economies, and the key factors affecting performance, so as to establish clear objectives for Government policies influencing the future development of rural economies.

Oversight of the Rural Economies project

Each team's work has been overseen by a sponsor Minister with an interest in (but no direct policy responsibility for) the subject area. The rural economies project sponsor Minister was Andrew Smith MP (formerly Minister of State at the Department for Education and Employment, now Chief Secretary to the Treasury). In addition, the project was greatly assisted by being able to draw on the experience and advice of its steering group. The group comprised:

- *David Baldock:* Director of the Institute for European Environmental Policy

- *Dudley Coates:* Ministry for Agriculture, Fisheries and Food

- *John Elvidge and Jim Gallagher:* Cabinet Office

- *Norman Glass:* Her Majesty's Treasury

- *Sir Simon Gourlay:* former President of the National Farmers Union

- *Sophia Lambert:* Department for Environment, Transport and the Regions

- *Liz Lloyd:* No 10 Policy Unit

- *Professor Sir John Marsh:* Retired Professor and former Head of Centre for Agricultural Strategy, University of Reading

- *Professor David Pearce:* University College London, Head of the Centre for Social and Economic Research on the Global Environment

- *Stephen Aldridge:* PIU Chief Economist

- *Suma Chakrabarti:* PIU Director

- *Greg Wilkinson:* PIU Project team leader

ANNEX A2: ARTICLE 33 MEASURES[1]

'Support shall be granted for measures, relating to farming activities and their conversion and to rural activities, which do not fall within the scope of any other measures referred to in this Title.

Such measures shall concern:

- Land improvement;

- Reparcelling;

- Setting up of farm relief and farm management services;

- Marketing of quality agricultural products;

- Basic services for the rural economy and population;

- Renovation and development of villages and protection and conservation of the rural heritage;

- Diversification of agricultural activities and activities close to agriculture, to provide multiple activities or alternative incomes;

- Agricultural water resources management;

- Development and improvement of infrastructure connected with the development of agriculture;

- Encouragement for tourist and craft activities;

- Protection of the environment in connection with land, forestry and landscape conservation as well as with the improvement of animal welfare;

- Restoring agricultural production potential damaged by natural disasters and introducing appropriate prevention measures;

- Financial engineering'.

[1] EU Commission DG6 (1999), *Council Regulation Number 1257/1999.*

ANNEX A3: RATIONALE AND PRINCIPLES FOR GOVERNMENT ACTION ON ECONOMIC MATTERS

In modern economies there is now a general presumption that markets are the most efficient mechanism for allocating resources and the most effective mechanism for creating and increasing national income.

This concept of economic efficiency includes environmental considerations and the need for sustainable development – to ensure a better quality of life for everyone, now and for generations to come. This requires a balance between economic growth and the prudent management of our resources – improving opportunities and social outcomes for everyone, protecting the environment and making efficient use of natural resources.

The presumption in favour of markets reflects a number of factors, including the fact that Government, like the market, can be imperfect and that there are costs as well as benefits to government intervention. Against this backdrop, the traditional rationale for government intervention rests on one or both of two arguments:

- that there are *market failures* which result in economic inefficiencies and which can be corrected or overcome through government intervention;

- that there are *distributional* considerations which justify government intervention irrespective of the efficiency or otherwise of market processes.

Market failure in rural areas is likely to be associated with four broad types of phenomenon – public goods, externalities, imperfect information and structural economic adjustment.

Public goods have two key defining features:

- they are not excludable, those that do not pay for a public good cannot be excluded from benefiting from it; and

- they are non-rival, each person consuming the public good does not diminish the ability of others to also consume that good.

From the definition it is clear that there are very few pure public goods. National defence is probably the closest example. However, there are many goods that have public good characteristics and so would typically be under-provided by the market (for example – in a rural context – fresh air and tranquillity, the diversity of species, and beautiful and irreplaceable landscapes). These are often known as 'club goods'. The enjoyment of a beautiful landscape like the Lake District is to some extent rival: as the number of people present increases, the enjoyment each gets from the tranquillity and the open spaces will decrease.

This has two implications. First, there will come a point at which the total enjoyment of everyone at that particular lake will fall when an additional person comes along – even though that person will still enjoy the landscape. In other words there is an optimal level of usage. Second, at this level, those currently enjoying the lake would be willing to pay enough to prevent a further person from enjoying it – as the potential decrease in their enjoyment is larger than the potential enjoyment that person could gain from the lake. At this point, those already enjoying the lake would benefit from forming a club to protect their enjoyment of the lake (hence club good).

Public and club goods have value but no market, or only an imperfect one. This value may arise from the use of such goods ('amenity value'), from the benefit people get from knowing such goods exist ('existence value'), and from safeguarding such goods for future uses which may presently be unknown ('option value').

This is scope for at least some private provision of goods with public good characteristics, for example the National Trust is a private body providing landscape and other environmental amenities. However, the inability to fully recoup the costs of this provision in many instances (because of incomplete excludability and/or rivalry) does imply that the market alone will under-provide these goods. Moreover, the exclusion implicit in financing private provision of club goods may conflict with other distributional objectives – if large sections of the population are priced out of enjoying the benefits of these goods.

Externalities are the external costs and benefits from an activity (to society as a whole) that are not reflected in the private costs and benefits experienced by the participants in that activity (producers and consumers). Markets will only work efficiently if producers and consumers bear the full costs of their production and consumption decisions and are fully rewarded for the benefits arising from their production and consumption decisions.

If there are external costs to production, the full cost to society will exceed the private cost to the producer. Thus the market signals to the producer will lead to excessive production, beyond the socially efficient level (taking account of the wider costs). Similarly if there are external benefits from a good, so that the social benefit exceeds the private

benefit to consumers, these external benefits will not be reflected in the price consumers are willing (individually) to pay, leading to under-provision of the good. For example, in the rural context, recreational users of the countryside (such as walkers, cyclists, and motorists) may not take account of the environmental damage they can create; and farmers may not recognise the wider environmental benefits (habitat and attractiveness) of their hedgerows when maintaining their fields.

Imperfect information is where one or more parties to a transaction are unaware of the full costs or benefits of their activities and/or the true nature of the product they are offering to buy or sell. Decisions taken by individuals in the absence of key relevant information may have large and potentially permanent adverse effects. For example, if Government does not know the true value of an environmental outcome (e.g. a particular habitat or species) then it may end up paying too much, or too little, in order to secure its conservation.

The market may be slow to bring about **structural economic adjustment** and in the process may impose excessive economic, social and other costs. The market adjustment process may be slow because of imperfections in the labour, capital and product markets. For example, imperfections in the housing market may hinder the movement of workers to where the jobs are.

The speed of the market adjustment process is important as delay may impose additional economic and social costs. For example, prolonged periods of economic inactivity or unemployment can erode skills and human capital, and can exacerbate problems of poverty and social exclusion. Also the adjustment process causes different groups to respond in different ways as the mobile and affluent can leave areas in decline while the immobile and less well-off cannot. As out-migration occurs, both public and private services and facilities may become increasingly under-utilised and the viability of whole communities may eventually be called into question.

Some rural areas and economies may have characteristics which give rise to exceptionally high adjustment costs. These characteristics include remoteness, which makes new business difficult to attract; and the high costs of new infrastructure reflecting the remoteness of the areas and the sparsity of the population.

Equity

Governments also have **distributional and equity objectives**, in addition to concerns about economic efficiency. Such distributional objectives are ultimately a matter of political judgement and may involve a trade-off with economic efficiency and growth. However, they have been a key reason for rural and agricultural policy and for government interventions in rural areas over many decades.

In the rural context, the distributional and equity objectives of policy have had two broad dimensions. At one level, they are about equity, or perceptions of equity, between rural and urban areas. Concerns about the alleged urban bias of current government policies and the desire to preserve the 'fabric of rural England' fall under this heading. At another level, they are about the poverty and social exclusion of deprived people. In this case, the concern is that some people in rural areas suffer disadvantage because of low incomes, poor housing, lack of access to services (such as transport, health care) and the absence of employment opportunities.

There has been increasing recognition in recent years that economic efficiency is not independent of distributional outcomes. It was noted above that, if structural economic adjustment exacerbates problems of poverty and social exclusion, this may jeopardise the efficient functioning of markets and local economies, for example because of the resulting social tensions and conflict, disaffection and apathy. This interdependence between economic efficiency and distributional equity is one element of what is referred to 'social capital' – a growing area of theory, building on the work of Robert Putnam and others.

Social capital consists of all those institutional arrangements, networks and relationships which promote understanding, trust and mutual respect; allow communities to pursue shared goals more effectively; improve information flows; and generally improve the quality of life. If, for example, trust is absent from social relationships the transaction and other costs of doing business will be higher than if it is present and markets will function less efficiently. Similarly, good social networks may, for example, facilitate the transmission of information about employment and business opportunities.

Government failure and the scope for government intervention

In reaching a decision on intervention, an analysis of government failure as well as market failure is crucial in coming to a view about the direction of policy. Government failure may arise through incentives to politicians and public servants to pursue inappropriate policies; through imperfect information or analysis; and through the unintended consequences of intervention. Government failure matters because intervention has costs whether because of regulatory burdens or because expenditure programmes have (ultimately) to be financed by distortionary taxes. Various policies, though desirable in their own terms, may have unintended detrimental effects on rural areas and economies – for example, planning policies require a trade-off between protection of the environment and economic development.

The recognition of the limits to government's role has driven the deregulation agenda and has encouraged a focus on the enabling role of government, rather than direct intervention. As there are few pure public goods (most are exclusive and/or rival in some way), there is scope for private provision which government can encourage and facilitate. For example, agri-environment schemes contribute towards the costs to farmers of maintaining environmental features that are no longer part of a purely efficient operation, such as dry-stone walls, hedgerows, and flower rich meadows.

Which instruments to use?

In deciding which instrument to use to tackle an environmental problem, it is necessary to weigh up the effectiveness of each in achieving the intended objectives against its economic, social or other costs. The aim should be to use the most cost-effective instrument for achieving the objectives of policy (where cost-effectiveness takes account of all these costs).

The instruments available to government, their strengths and weaknesses and the circumstances in which it is appropriate to use them are discussed below. There are some disadvantages common to all the instruments listed. These reflect the risks of inefficiencies inherent in intervention by government and include:

- Potentially harmful redistribution (of income, property rights, etc) if instruments are poorly targeted;

- The risk that market structures may allow the impact of the intervention to be passed on (e.g. from producers to consumers);

- The risk of creating unintended distortions to economic activity (beyond the intended effects of the intervention) because it is difficult to measure desired outcomes which results on a focus on inputs and intermediary stages; and

- Markets are innovative and will devote significant efforts to minimising the impact of the interference (e.g. the tax avoidance industry).

(a) regulatory instruments such as the planning system

Regulation is the use of legislation or other statutory instruments or powers to constrain or set conditions for the activities of an individual, firm or other organisation. The advantages of regulation as an instrument for furthering environmental objectives are that it is:

- relatively easy for government to impose and target;

- good for setting enforcing minimum standards, and at preventing particularly undesirable activities; and

- less costly in terms of public expenditure than some other instruments (e.g. subsidies/incentive payments), though they may have significant enforcement costs.

The disadvantages are that it:

- can impose a heavy burden of compliance costs on the regulated and may have significant effects on competition and innovation (economic dynamism) – although it can also encourage innovation to meet regulatory standards;

- relies on the polluter for information which makes it difficult to determine appropriate targets and performance against them; and

- can discourage or prevent undesirable activities but it is more difficult to encourage positive ones (e.g. planting new hedgerows) though they may be able to encourage a relative shift in priorities.

(b) taxes and charges

A tax or charge is a mandatory payment by an individual, firm or other organisation to central or local government. The advantages of taxes and charges as instruments for furthering environmental objectives are that they:

- can help ensure that economic agents face the full costs of their actions and thus have a continuing incentive to reduce activities which (e.g.) damage the environment;

- give those paying the tax flexibility in how they respond (compared with regulatory interventions) which should reduce the overall cost to society of achieving environmental and other objectives; and

- may raise revenue which creates scope for the reduction of other (distortionary) taxes.

The main disadvantages are:

- determining the level at which the tax or charge is set. In principle, it ought to be related to the damage done by the activity subject to the tax or charge but this may be difficult to measure;

- it may be impractical to apply charges (for example on diffuse pollution of watercourses by farmers);

- it is much easier to discourage harmful activities than to encourage positive ones: tax relief is only effective for those already paying tax, although it may be able to encourage a relative shift in priorities.

(c) public spending – subsidies, incentive payments etc

A subsidy or incentive payment may be defined as any fiscal instrument by which government provides financial assistance to individuals or organisations for a specific activity. The advantages of subsidies are they can:

- be used to promote beneficial activities of various kinds;

- encourage innovation if subsidies support the development of new techniques; and

- serve a redistributive function.

The disadvantages are that:

- they may distort the pattern of economic activity causing inefficiencies rather than an improved allocation of resources, e.g. by creating dependence on the subsidy if it is open-ended rather than time-limited or transitional;

- they need to be financed, e.g. by taxes that are themselves distortionary.

Conventional wisdom on government action

Reflecting these different types of instrument and their relative merits, there are a variety of measures that government can take to address the different forms of market failure and its distributional objectives. These include:

- act as the 'provider of last resort' for public goods, for example through the National Parks and Forestry Commission;

- use and enforce legislation to protect and preserve public goods, for example the use of SSSIs and listed buildings;

- encourage and facilitate private provision of public goods, for example the National Trust;

- reflect the wider costs and benefits to society of an activity in its price, through taxes and charges;

- assist markets to price wider costs and benefits to society of an activity, for example through tradeable quotas and permits;

- provide and facilitate access to information;

- provide a regulatory safety net, for example health, safety and quality standards; and addressing market power and abuse;

- build the capacity of communities to help themselves, with government, whether central, regional or local, playing a partnership role;

- use taxation and public spending to redistribute income.

Summary: not by economics alone

This rationale for intervention – and the recognition of its limitations – must influence whatever is to replace the post-war paradigm for rural policy. But government cannot operate by economic insight alone. The new arrangements must be derived not only from economic theory but also from an analysis of rural problems and opportunities and, most importantly, from an overall vision of what the Government values about – and wants from – rural areas.